100 THINGS
FALCONS FANS
SHOULD KNOW & DO
BEFORE THEY DIE

100 THINGS
FALCONS FANS
SHOULD KNOW & DO
BEFORE THEY DIE

Ray Glier and Knox Bardeen

TRIUMPH
BOOKS

Library of Congress Cataloging-in-Publication Data

Glier, Ray.
  100 things Falcons fans should know & do before they die / Ray Glier and Knox Bardeen.
     p. cm.
  Includes bibliographical references.
  ISBN 978-1-60078-725-6 (pbk.)
  1. Atlanta Falcons (Football team)—History. 2. Atlanta Falcons (Football team)—Miscellanea. I. Bardeen, Knox. II. Title. III. Title: One hundred things Falcons fans should know & do before they die.
  GV956.A85G55 2012
  796.332'6409758231—dc23
                                     2012023409

This book is available in quantity at special discounts for your group or organization. For further information, contact:
  Triumph Books LLC
  814 North Franklin Street
  Chicago, Illinois 60610
  (312) 337-0747
  www.triumphbooks.com

Printed in U.S.A.
ISBN: 978-1-60078-725-6
Design by Patricia Frey
Photos courtesy of AP Images unless otherwise indicated

To Jeff Van Note—A Hall of Famer in this book.
—Ray Glier

To my wife, Jennifer, and my children,
Anna and Knox, who happily put up with all my
late dinners, missed bedtimes, and Sunday
afternoons away from home. I love you all!
—Knox Bardeen

Contents

Acknowledgments

Writing a book is no easy task, and it's not enough that a writer takes his own time to jot down his thoughts, come up with a plan, and strategize about what to include. Writing a book like this would never be possible without a lot of help. If not for many gracious hours from players, coaches, and members of the Falcons staff, there's no way these words would ever have made the pages you're reading now. If not for the love and support of family, none of this would have come to fruition.

From Knox:

Thank you to the Atlanta Falcons football communications staff: Reggie Roberts, Frank Kleha, Brian Cearns, and Matt Haley. You guys have answered a billion questions (I only slightly exaggerate) and never once threatened to kick me out if I didn't stop asking.

A special thanks to Frank Kleha, who took time from his busy schedule on multiple occasions to take me places and show me pieces of Falcons history that very few people get to see. Your keen grasp of the history of this team shows in a number of places in this book.

Matt Moore, the Falcons video services coordinator—who has as much fun with his job as anyone on the planet—smiled the whole time he was sharing some of his favorite stories from his work.

Thanks to D. Orlando Ledbetter, the great *Atlanta-Journal Constitution* writer, who never once shied away from guiding me as I learned the ropes around Flowery Branch. No one has taught me more about the ins and outs of covering an NFL team than "D-Led."

Thank you, Jay Adams and Daniel Cox, two of the key cogs in the AtlantaFalcons.com machine, who always make my time covering the team more enjoyable.

And to Jason Butt of CBS Sports, who started covering the Falcons with me on the same day but has since moved on to the Baltimore Ravens. The fact that you still answer my calls and help me on a daily basis from 700 miles away amazes me.

To John Michaels, John Manasso, and Hans Heiserer, more members of the local media, who stand around, rain or shine, and watch tons and tons of Falcons practice snaps with me, all the while allowing me to bounce ideas around. Thank you for listening.

Thank you to Dave Choate and Alex Welch, exceptionally knowledgeable Falcons writers, who both allowed me to bounce ideas off them and helped me determine what fans would want to read about.

And to the many interview subjects, players, and coaches from both the past and present who allowed me the time needed over the years to gain enough insight to write this book.

Thank you, Knox and Gloria Bardeen, my parents, whose countless hours coaching, officiating, and mending during my years as a youth athlete helped to turn me into the sports enthusiast I am today.

And a special thank you to Tom Herrera, my first boss at FanHouse, whose enthusiastic interest in developing new writing talent opened the door to my first job writing about professional football. The fact that you took so much time to assist me in honing my writing skills and cared so much about the direction of my career will never be forgotten.

Introduction

When Ray approached me to collaborate on this book with him, I immediately thought it was a great idea, and not just because I've always wanted to write a book.

Ray's been in this business for a long time, and he's had his finger on the pulse of Atlanta sports for years. He was around during the Mike Vick years, he's visited multiple Falcons training camps in multiple locations, and he's built relationships with former Falcons stars. All these experiences were invaluable in putting this book together and shine brightly on the pages within.

I, on the other hand, am relatively new to the Atlanta sports scene but have been entrenched with the Falcons for three years. I've built a strong relationship with the team and the current players, and my intimate knowledge of this regime that comes from being in Flowery Branch every day from August to February helped dramatically.

In a sense, we're the literary version of a running backs corps that features a two-headed monster. One of us is the power runner while the other works as the change-of-pace back. The symbiotic relationship works well, and everyone benefits.

So sit back and enjoy these 100 things every Falcons fan should know and do. We sure enjoyed writing them. The combination of history with the present, the melding of personal insight with research, and the delicate balance between things to know and things to do will be a great way to pass the time while you're not watching the Falcons on Sundays.

—Knox Bardeen

1 Finally, a Super Day

OK, it didn't end so super. The Falcons got to the Super Bowl and were drubbed 34–19 by the Denver Broncos.

So what's worse, never getting to the big stage, or having a bad day when the lights come on? Never getting there is much worse, of course.

The game in south Florida was a bar-raising event for the franchise, which had been stuck in a rut of ridicule for most of its 33 seasons. Until, that is, this 1998 team went 16–3 with a physical style of football that was to run first and knock opponents silly on defense.

The Falcons lost the Super Bowl but still had a parade. Hell, yeah. Why not have a parade? The team was 8–0 at home in the Georgia Dome and 14–2 overall in the regular season, which were firsts for the franchise. Dan Reeves, the head coach, had heart surgery in the middle of the season and then returned to coach the club to the NFC title.

It was a team that controlled the ball and took the ball from the other team. They scored a team-record 442 points and led the NFL with 44 takeaways.

"If the ball is not on the ground, we will knock the [stuff] out of somebody," said defensive end Chuck Smith. "We are not prima donnas. We will get after people. You get hit hard enough, believe me, you will let go of the ball. There's nobody in this game that can't be shaken up, nobody who can't be hurt, nobody who cannot lose the ball."

The team had an effervescent star in running back Jamal Anderson, with his gleaming smile and legs that moved like a sewing machine as he cut through the line. Anderson rushed for 1,846 yards and had an NFL-high 12 100-yard rushing games.

Anderson also had the best footwork in the team's trademark dance, the Dirty Bird, which became a symbol of the team's fun style. One of the highlights of the season was Reeves, the old-school coach, dancing the Dirty Bird with Anderson as the team was presented the NFC championship trophy following the win over the Vikings.

Reeves was named Coach of the Year for taking the team to just its second division title in 33 years and living to tell about it following his heart episode.

But the Falcons could not finish the drill in the Super Bowl. They had their chances with four possessions inside the Denver 30-yard line in the first half but scored just six points. This was an offense that knew how to finish in the other team's territory. Quarterback Chris Chandler, inside an opponent's 20-yard line, had zero interceptions during the regular season. He had 16 touchdown passes, but he could not make the big throw that would get the Falcons some early traction.

The Broncos crossed up the Atlanta defense with an empty-set backfield. The Birds were spread out, and quarterback John Elway picked them apart, but he also made deep throws to beat ambitious Atlanta safeties who were trying to make the big play on the big stage.

"I'm going to keep my head up no matter what," said cornerback Ray Buchanan, who had guaranteed that the Falcons would win. "The Lord blessed this football team to come from ground zero to play in the Super Bowl…. I'm not going to apologize. I had the guarantee and the confidence that this football team could win. There was no doubt in my mind. I'll never take that back."

The loss was a sour end to the biggest week in franchise history. It was made worse when safety Eugene Robinson, who had preached that his team needed to take a business-style approach to the Super Bowl, was arrested for offering an undercover officer $40 for sex. Robinson had received the Bart Starr Award for community service during Super Bowl week, only to be caught on a Miami street soliciting sex.

The next day, the game was played and the Falcons were humbled. But they had gotten there. They had millions of eyeballs on them. Cher sang and Stevie Wonder danced, and all the glory was around the Dirty Birds.

The stage was theirs. The spotlights were wheeled in. It didn't end well, but at least there is a story to tell.

2 A Super Kick

Morten Andersen was walking through the Falcons' parking lot at the team's complex in Suwanee on a Monday afternoon when a reporter (me) approached.

"Nice kick," I said, referring to the field goal that beat Minnesota in the NFC Championship Game.

"Thanks," Andersen said.

"Nice paycheck," I said.

Then a smile creased his face. "How did you hear about it?" he asked. A moment later, he said, "That's between me and the club."

Then he smiled again.

That field goal was a hole in one...with a broken club, in a stiff wind, in pouring rain. That was the kick of a career, and that's saying something when you consider the peaks in Mort's career.

When Andersen kicked the 38-yard field goal in overtime that beat the Minnesota Vikings on January 17, 1999, he immediately became $300,000 richer, due to a stipulation in his contract written in by him and agent Greg Campbell. In 1999 $300 grand for a kick was a really sweet deal, but in order for the rider in the contract to kick in, so to speak, it had to be in a conference championship game and it had to be a game-winner.

In other words, the kick had to have substance. Getting the Falcons into the Super Bowl had substance. Andersen actually made $332,500 that day because a winner's share of playoff money for that game was $32,500. Peanuts.

Andersen called it the biggest kick he had made in 17 years. Well, yeah.

I haven't seen the contract, but I'm wondering if the kick clause was written in the margins, in red ink, with a smiley face where the period should have been: "By the way, if Morten Andersen, kicker, ever boots this franchise into the Super Bowl (fat chance) he gets an additional $300,000."

"I actually forgot about the clause in the contract," Andersen said in December 2011. "It was the Santa Clause."

The Falcons' Andersen got a chance at the huge payday because his pal on the Vikings, Gary Anderson, missed a fourth-quarter field goal in the NFC Championship Game that would have pushed the Vikings out to a 10-point lead in the fourth quarter. As it was, a limping Chris Chandler took the Falcons downfield for a tying touchdown, and then Gary Anderson missed and Morten Andersen made, and there was a party on the field.

Ten years later, Gary Anderson, who was still kicking in the NFL, raised an eyebrow when told about the bonus. "I didn't know that," he said.

"You made it possible," I said.

"Don't remind me," Gary said. He smiled. He was happy for Mort.

Andersen and Anderson shared more than similar last names. They came from abroad—Andersen from Denmark, Anderson from South Africa—to have sensational NFL careers as soccer-style

Getting His Kicks

Morten Andersen was around long enough to influence all kinds of Falcons records for a kicker. Here are some statistics he is a part of and some he is not.

The most points in Falcons history: Morten Andersen leads with 806, way ahead of Mick Luckhurst, who has 558. Jay Feely, another kicker, comes in at 436. Then there's Terance Mathis, the wide receiver, at 354. Then comes Andre Rison at 338.

Here are some lists of other Mort stats. He could kick for average, he could kick for distance. He could just plain kick. All you had to do was look at Mort's legs as he ran out to attempt a kick. They were thick, like a cannon's tube.

Most FGs Made, Career
184 Morten Andersen (1995–2000, 2006–07)
115 Mick Luckhurst (1981–87)
98 Jay Feely (2001–04)

Most FGs Made, Season
32 Jay Feely (2002)
31 Morten Andersen (1995)
29 Jason Elam (2008)
29 Jay Feely (2001)

Most FGs Made, Game
6 Norm Johnson (11/13/94)
6 Morten Andersen (10/1/06)

Most FGs Attempted, Career
224 Morten Andersen (1995–2000, 2006–07)
164 Mick Luckhurst (1981–87)
127 Jay Feely (2001–04)

Best FG Percentage, Career (Min. 35)
.866 Norm Johnson (84 of 97) (1991–94)
.853 Matt Bryant (35 of 41) (2009–10)
.821 Morten Andersen (184 of 224) (1995–2000, 2006–07)
.772 Jay Feely (98 of 127) (2001–04)

kickers. They battled each other the last several years of their career to see who would be the all-time leading scorer in NFL history. Mort leads with 2,544. Gary is second with 2,434.

"The Great Dane," as Andersen is called, made 79.7 percent of his field goals. He was brought back to the Falcons in 2007 and was more than a stopgap. He made 25 of 28 field goals.

Just as impressive as a near 80 percent mark is the fact that Andersen is the all-time leading scorer for two teams: the Saints and the Falcons. Andersen was looking for one more contract in 2008 and would have become the oldest player ever in the NFL if a team had signed him, but he retired in December 2008 without a deal.

Everybody who has ever kicked a football in the NFL would be happy for Mort. So many games in the NFL are decided by a late field goal, and kickers do not get their just due. Matt Bryant, the current Falcons kicker—and as clutch a kicker as there is in football these days—just had one word for Andersen's $300,000 boot: "Nice."

The 1998 Season: The Games That Led to the Super Bowl Run

When Falcons fans get together and talk about the history of their team—the ups and downs, the brightest and darkest days—one year is sure to stand out in everyone's mind: 1998. Sure there have been several memorable periods throughout Atlanta's past. The first playoff appearance is 1978 was a groundbreaking moment for everyone involved with or a fan of the organization. The Gritz Blitz squad of 1977 was another team that will always be recognized, along with more recent seasons under the new regime of Mike

Smith and Matt Ryan. No matter where you go or who you talk to, though, you'll always hear a reference to the 1998 season, the most successful year in the history of the Falcons franchise.

Overall, the 1990s were quite a bipolar stage for the Falcons. In 1991 they finished 10–6 and went on to reach the NFC divisional playoffs. Next came three consecutive years of records below .500, followed by another playoff appearance in 1995. In 1996 Atlanta completely fell of the map, dropping 13 games in the regular season to mark the worst performance since 1989. The team was 7–9 in 1997, nothing extremely dreadful but nothing to write home about either. But what transpired the following season completely baffled everyone but proved the most pleasant surprise Falcons fans could ever receive. Dan Reeves was in his second year as head coach. Quarterback Chris Chandler was coming off a Pro Bowl season despite the team's unimpressive record. Jamal Anderson had rushed for 1,002 yards in 1997, but his 3.5 yards per carry didn't really blow anyone away. In other words, nothing had radically changed from 1997. There was talent on the roster, undoubtedly, but no one could have anticipated a Super Bowl run. That's right, the Falcons defied all odds in 1998 and made it to the team's first-ever Super Bowl, but it was anything but a simple task to get there.

Atlanta opened up the season on the road against Kerry Collins and the Carolina Panthers. They edged out a tight contest and came away with a 1–0 start to the year, defeating the recent expansion team 19–14. The following week was the first home game for the Falcons, and yet again they managed to stick out a close one, besting Philadelphia with a final of 17–12. The defense appeared to be solid in the opening weeks, but nothing about the team screamed "Super Bowl contender."

Week 3 was a bye week, and a Week 4 divisional trip to San Francisco set the Falcons back to 2–1, as Steve Young and the 49ers offense put up 31 points and looked just as good as their 13–3 team from the season prior.

Week 5 changed things a bit, however, as Atlanta took on Carolina again and completely tore apart the young squad, winning 51–23. The Falcons offense looked impressive, and they did not disappoint very often, going forward. Atlanta won the next two contests and found itself with a 5–1 record.

Just when things were starting to pick up, a setback occurred before the Falcons' October 25 matchup against the New York Jets. Chandler was unable to play due to injury, leaving the Falcons to depend on backup Steve DeBerg to lead the offense. The end result was not pretty. Atlanta dropped its second game of the year 28–3, faltering entirely without the likes of Chandler running the show.

Chandler wasn't out for long, fortunately for Atlanta, and things were back on track the next week. A 37–15 victory over St. Louis put the team at 6–2, and they were on a course to take on the New England Patriots the next week. The Falcons truly looked like a team capable of a playoff run against the Patriots, sparking one of the most electrifying games they played all year. Chandler and Anderson piled on the points, the defense refused to budge, and when it was all said and done, the Falcons walked away with a remarkable 41–10 victory. From there on out there was no stopping the Dirty Birds.

Jamal Anderson did the Dirty Bird dance often in 1998, as he rushed for 14 touchdowns for the year. With their young running back dancing all over the place and a veteran quarterback looking sharper than ever, the Falcons managed to defeat every opponent they faced after that second loss to the Jets. They won nine games to close out the regular season, and the city of Atlanta had no idea how to feel, for all of Georgia had never seen any kind of success like this as far as professional football went.

If you lived in Atlanta during the finest run in Falcons history, you know just how ecstatic the entire region was. One couldn't travel anywhere in Georgia without seeing Falcons logos, flags, jerseys, and myriad other items bearing the team's iconography.

The fan base had been awaiting a season like this one for quite some time—32 years, to be exact.

The Falcons forged ahead into the playoffs. With a first-round bye, they took on none other than the 49ers in the divisional round of the playoffs. One of Atlanta's two losses had been to San Francisco, but they avenged that initial defeat in Week 11. This was the rubber match of the season series, and how fitting it was.

Jamal Anderson led the way once again, assaulting the Niners defense for 113 rushing yards and two touchdowns. Steve Young and Jerry Rice attempted to finish the game with some last-minute heroics, but they came up short. Atlanta came away on top 20–18 and headed to the NFC Championship Game, the first conference championship the Falcons had ever been involved in.

Despite all the success the Dirty Birds had seen in 1998, there were very few souls on this earth who expected them to beat the 16–1 Minnesota Vikings to go to the Super Bowl. Randall Cunningham piloted one of the most powerful offenses in all of football, with Cris Carter, Randy Moss, and Robert Smith backing him up. All four players were Pro Bowlers that year, and the Vikings had 10 players total on the Pro Bowl roster, just to give an idea of what the Falcons were up against.

Minnesota jumped out to an early lead at home in the Hubert H. Humphrey Metrodome. The Vikings led 20–7 in the second quarter, but Chandler managed to put his team right back in the mix. Terance Mathis caught a touchdown pass to make it 20–14 heading into halftime.

Morten Andersen kicked a 27-yard field goal with 5:36 left in the third quarter, putting Atlanta just three points behind in the never-ending uphill battle. The Vikings remained indifferent to any comeback attempt and marched right back 82 yards in 15 plays for a Matthew Hatchette touchdown catch, putting the score at 27–17.

Chandler followed up that drive with a 70-yard completion to Tony Martin, and Andersen booted a 35-yarder to bring the

Falcons within seven. The ensuing possession from the Vikings, though, provided one of the most unbelievable moments of the entire season.

Cunningham managed to take the Vikings down to Atlanta's end zone once again, but when the drive stalled, they were forced to kick a field goal. The Vikings' Gary Anderson had been automatic all season long. In fact, he hadn't missed all year. A 38-yard kick seemed like a simple chip shot for a guy this clutch. And then, with one swift, untimely miss, the Metrodome crowd was completely stunned. Anderson had missed, and the Falcons took over on downs. He hadn't missed in 46 consecutive attempts. No one could believe it. It was a bad dream for Vikings fans, and they couldn't wake up.

The Falcons drove down the field and tied up the game, and the rest is history. Atlanta found itself with a game-winning opportunity, and their Andersen connected on a field goal to send the Falcons to the Super Bowl.

Their run finally came to an end at the hands of John Elway and the Denver Broncos, but it was a moment that no fan in Atlanta will ever forget. It was almost unfathomable that the Falcons could even make it to the NFC Championship Game, let alone win the thing. They lost 34–19 in Super Bowl XXXIII, but hope had been sparked. It was possible for this franchise to make it to the end of the road, a fact that fans will never forget.

The Smiths Made It Happen

Before there was Mike Smith, there was Rankin M. Smith Sr., Rankin Smith Jr., and Taylor Smith. Mike Smith would not be here without the other Smiths. Say a thank-you to Rankin Smith. He got the Falcons here, at least.

Atlanta becomes a full-fledged member of the National Football League! Then-commissioner Pete Rozelle, left, presented a certificate of membership to Rankin Smith Sr. on February 15, 1966.

On June 30, 1965, Rankin M. Smith Sr. was awarded a National Football League franchise for $8.5 million, the largest price ever paid for a professional franchise. Smith intended to start an American Football League franchise until the NFL showed up at his doorstep and he changed his mind and joined the bigger, better league. Smith already had the rights to use Atlanta–Fulton County Stadium and all the leverage he needed. "Doesn't every adult male in America want to own his own football team?" he asked at the time.

The Falcons had their first team in 1966, and the fans flocked to Atlanta–Fulton County Stadium for the first season. They were

3–11 and played before crowds that averaged 56,526 people per game.

The Falcons and Smith won their first game on November 20 against the New York Giants in Yankee Stadium. They were the only expansion team in NFL history, at the time, not to finish in last place. Smith's first draft pick, Tommy Nobis, had a sensational rookie year and was voted to the Pro Bowl, and then...well...disappointment followed.

The Falcons slid along for years. They would improve, then drop off, improve, then drop off. They never had back-to-back winning seasons under Smith's ownership. He died in 1997 at 72 years old, and Taylor Smith took over the team until the family sold the team in 2002 for $545 million to Arthur Blank, an Atlantan and graduate of the University of Georgia.

Smith was as responsible as anyone for getting the Georgia Dome built. He did it the old-fashioned way...with leverage. He threatened to move the team if he could not get some relief from the outdated Atlanta Stadium. The Falcons finally moved to the new stadium in 1992.

On cue, the NFL rewarded Smith with a Super Bowl hosting gig in 1993. The Falcons hosted another in 2000. Smith was an influential owner but not a terribly successful one in terms of wins and losses. He served on the NFL's expansion committee, which awarded franchises to Southern-based teams in Charlotte and Jacksonville.

The Falcons did not make the playoffs until 1978 and had a losing record in 22 of the 31 seasons Smith was alive and running the franchise. Atlanta made five playoff appearances and won the NFC West title in 1980, but Smith was ridiculed over and over for his downtrodden franchise.

"If you took all this stuff to heart, you'd go crazy," Smith told the *AJC* in 1994. "You listen to the [radio] talk shows, and that stuff is just [baloney].... I think when you're in this business, there's no question it's life in a fishbowl. And sometimes, you've just got to swim away."

Len Pasquarelli, the former Falcons beat writer for the *AJC*, said Smith was not one to cut and run. His fellow NFL owners also understood the man was not going to be broken by losing football games.

"With some owners, you see the frustration build up, and you wonder if they can withstand the pressure," Cleveland Browns and Baltimore Ravens owner Art Modell told Pasquarelli. "I don't think any of us have ever questioned the resolve or the staying power of Rankin."

The measure of the man was not in the futile chase for a championship for the Falcons. He was much more than the Falcons' owner, who hired and fired coaches and tried to keep the franchise on the tracks. The record was 176–291–5 under Smith, but as Steve Hummer of the *Atlanta Journal-Constitution* wrote following Smith's death, "Smith was a civic treasure."

Smith donated to the Fernbank Museum of Natural History and led a fund-raising drive that brought in $43 million. The IMAX Theater at Fernbank is named in honor of Smith.

In 1985 Smith founded the Atlanta Falcons Youth Foundation, which Blank has turned into one of the most generous philanthropic foundations in all of pro sports.

Smith's family did not let the generosity melt away when Rankin Smith Sr. died. They donated another $3.5 million to the University of Georgia, which was used for a student-athlete academic center.

The Gritz Blitz: Best Defense Ever?

Atlanta was still a fairly young team when 1977 rolled around. After starting up in 1966, the Falcons had seen two seasons with records over .500, but for the most part they really had yet to see any true success, at least as far as standards go for a consistently successful franchise.

But the Falcons were marauders in 1977, and never was a 7–7 team more feared. They came from all angles, and sometimes they would come nine at a time in a blitz called "the Sticky Sam." It was the first season of coach Leeman Bennett, and he instilled an attitude in the Falcons that had been rarely seen in the 11 years of the franchise.

It was the Gritz Blitz.

Alongside Bennett was Jerry Glanville, the man often credited with the success of the Gritz Blitz. The Falcons had made some big changes within the organization, and these new additions would prove to bring about one of the most historic seasons in the team's history.

They gave up 9.2 points per game, best in the NFL. Only three times did that team give up more than 300 yards per game.

Defensive end Claude Humphrey was still a star for the Falcons and settled down after initial demands to be traded. Fulton Kuykendall was on that team. So was linebacker Robert Pennywell. Rolland Lawrence was a big-time player in the secondary. Rick Byas was another secondary standout.

How good was the chemistry of that defense? Linebacker Greg Brezina was an 11th-round pick out of Houston, but he was one of the standouts of that team, even in his ninth season in the NFL.

The defense simply had to be good because quarterback Steve Bartkowski was sidelined the first half of the season with a knee injury. The Falcons averaged just 13 points per game. Bartkowski started seven games, but he was a sitting duck in the pocket and was sacked 29 times, which is a beating. Scott Hunter started the other seven games and completed 46.4 percent of his throws and was sacked 11 times, but the Falcons did not have a lot of weapons on offense.

Without their young star QB, the Falcons had to step things up on the other side of the ball. It was up to the defense to make plays…and it did. Glanville implemented packages and blitz schemes that ultimately led to the heralded nickname sticking with the team throughout the years. Atlanta clearly didn't have the top talent in the league at the time, but these constant blitzing patterns drove offenses mad while providing a way to best utilize the players at hand.

The defense came up with 26 interceptions. That is nothing compared to the fumbles it forced and recovered. The opponents had the ball come loose 35 times, and the Falcons recovered 22.

The Gritz Blitz shut out two opponents and held two others to a field goal. If an opponent is held to 21 points in today's NFL, the defense has done a pretty fair job. The Gritz Blitz routinely held opponents to less than 21 points.

The Falcons played the Rams in the first game of the season, and veteran quarterback Joe Namath saw no dilemma in the Falcons' chaotic defense. On the first series of the season, he took the Rams down the field for a touchdown.

"You know, I came to Atlanta from the Rams," said Leeman Bennett, the Falcons coach. "It sure didn't look good that first series, but you know what? They didn't get anything after that." The Falcons defeated the Rams 17–6.

If there had been a better offense to go with the defense, the Falcons would have been a handful and gone into the playoffs.

Atlanta managed more than 300 yards in just two games. A familiar chorus could be heard at Atlanta–Fulton County Stadium: cheers for the defense, boos for the offense.

When the defense beat up Tampa Bay on November 27, the playoffs were in sight. The Falcons were 6–5 following the 17–0 win. They mauled the hapless Bucs, who were in just their second season. Tampa managed just 78 yards total offense, and its quarterbacks completed just five of 23 passes.

The next-best game for the defense was the 7–0 win at San Francisco on October 9, when the Falcons sacked the 49ers quarterbacks four times and gave up just 70 yards passing. San Francisco had Scott Bull at quarterback and also the former Heisman winner Jim Plunkett of Stanford, and with the loss yardage for sacks taken away from the passing numbers, the 49ers had a grand total of 35 yards with the passing game.

John James punted eight times for the Falcons in that game, but it hardly mattered. Not with the Gritz Blitz beating up the 49ers.

That's how it went all season. It got to the point where fans didn't mind some punts just to see Bennett unleash the furious defense on an opponent.

The Falcons set a new record for a 14-game season, giving up only 129 points. They allowed the fewest first downs (192) and fewest passing yards (1,384). Pittsburgh had its Steel Curtain, but the Gritz Blitz gave up just five rushing touchdowns all seasons.

But the offense was a ball and chain the defense had to drag around. After the 17–0 win over Tampa, the Falcons lost to the Patriots and the Rams. The playoffs were out of their grasp, but football had come alive under Bennett, Glanville, and the Gritz Blitz. Bennett was named United Press International's Coach of the Year, and Atlanta had a professional football team to be proud of.

Was this the best defense of all time, though? While critics argue the fact that it was a different age for the NFL, one that relied more on the run game, the Gritz Blitz squad is commonly considered one of the premier defenses in the chronicles of pro football.

The Falcons still hold the all-time record for fewest points allowed in a 14-game season. Claude Humphrey, Rolland Lawrence, and punter John James were all named to the Pro Bowl, providing a little more to celebrate after a .500 season.

As far as records go, the 1977 Falcons bested the 2000 Baltimore Ravens club in the majority of categories, including yards and points allowed per game. The Ravens defense fueled the team to a Super Bowl win in 2000 and is commonly referenced when discussing the greatest defenses ever.

The two teams are from different eras, and the game of football has radically changed over the years, but there's no disputing the 1977 Atlanta Falcons possessed one of the best defenses of all time. If the team had been able to do more on offense and perhaps even make a run in the playoffs, the Gritz Blitz club would probably have taken the title hands down.

Listen to Jessie "the Hammer" Tuggle

When Jessie Tuggle talks, you should stop what you're doing and listen.

When Tuggle is in any room, it's very easy to gravitate toward the former Atlanta Falcons linebacker. He constantly has a smile on his face, and he's always willing to share a story from his 14 years with the Falcons, and these stories usually have an inspirational twist involved.

Tuggle wasn't a prototypical linebacker—or football player, for that matter. At 5'11" and 230 pounds, many thought Tuggle was too small and slow to play in the NFL. That's why the Valdosta State graduate went undrafted in 1987.

The Falcons gave Tuggle a shot, and he turned on his high-octane engine and never turned it off. His 2,065 career tackles is a Falcons franchise record but not his most amazing feat on defense.

Tuggle, as an undrafted free agent, led the NFL in tackles over a 10-year period, from 1990 to 1999, with 1,293. The next-closest defensive player, Junior Seau, had 1,041.

Tuggle recorded 12 consecutive 100-tackle seasons and even notched two 200-tackle seasons. On four occasions Tuggle made 20 or more tackles in a single game, a 24-stop game his career best.

He was nicknamed "the Hammer" because of his penetrating hits and awesome power. Tuggle often said his nickname came from one specific task: "nailing people." Tuggle "nailed" enough running backs to be selected to Pro Bowl teams five times during his career.

Now 47, Tuggle talks about courage, drive, and never stopping, no matter what people say.

According to a *Griffin Daily News* report, when Tuggle was speaking at a local school, the former linebacker talked about overcoming obstacles. "People tell you, 'You can't do it,' [but] you've got to believe in yourself. I would have played for free if they had asked me to…. Don't be afraid to succeed. Don't be afraid to fail, because sometimes you are stronger afterward. Don't be afraid to make your mark at something you want to do," Tuggle advised.

Whether to schoolkids, local civic groups, or even current members of the Falcons organization, Tuggle always hands out advice when asked.

Speaking to the entire linebackers corps in 2011 prior to a game against New Orleans, Tuggle talked about a game in 1991 when he pounded out 22 tackles against the Saints.

"I know you guys have New Orleans this week," Tuggle started. "In 1991 we went into New Orleans, and I knocked down 22 tackles. After that, you know how you leave a game and you want to leave it all on the field? I left it all on the football field."

Tuggle left games in total exhaustion but didn't care. In his mind that's how a football player should feel after a game.

It came down for Tuggle, and still does, to taking advantage of every moment. The Hammer lived every waking moment like it was a gift. He seized opportunities that were laid in front of him and created some for himself.

It was all about heart and determination for Tuggle during his 14-year career...that and "nailing" a lot of people. He made the most out of his time in the league and now inspires others to do that same.

Listen to Jessie Tuggle when he talks about inspiration.

The Falcons-Saints Rivalry

The Atlanta–New Orleans rivalry certainly ranks as one of the most underrated and unheralded rivalries in not only the NFL, but all of sports.

There's an undying hatred between the two teams, dating back to when New Orleans entered the NFL in 1967. The timing of the two teams entering the NFL may have been the biggest contributor to the rivalry being born. But the two teams became natural rivals, given the proximity between their cities in the Deep South. (Dallas traditionally is considered southwest, and Washington is too far north.)

In the rivalry's early days, the game was dubbed the "Dixie Championship" by newspapers across the country. After spending its inaugural season in the Eastern Conference, Atlanta was moved to the Western Conference, which New Orleans also became a part of. Since 1967, Atlanta and New Orleans have played 95 regular-season games and once in the playoffs. Heading into the 2012 season, Atlanta held a 45–40 regular-season advantage over New Orleans and won the only playoff meeting between the two teams 27–20 in 1991 (more on that shortly).

"Every year, bus caravans loaded with rowdy (and usually very inebriated) fans make the seven-hour trip between the two cities," wrote sportswriter Len Pasquarelli for ESPN.com in 2006. "Unless you've attended a Falcons-Saints debauchery-filled afternoon, you'll just have to take my word for how much fun it really can be."

The first meeting between these two teams was on November 26, 1967, in New Orleans. The game was going Atlanta's way early as the Falcons jumped out to a 21–3 lead in the second quarter, thanks to a 32-yard halfback pass from Perry Lee Dunn to Tommy McDonald and a five-yard touchdown throw from quarterback Randy Johnson to Bill Martin. Before those two scores, Falcons running back Junior Coffey punched in a one-yard score.

But New Orleans answered before the first half ended, with Saints quarterback Gary Cuozzo hooking up with tight end Kent Kramer for a seven-yard score to cut Atlanta's lead to 21–10. In the third quarter Saints running back Randy Schultz scored a touchdown from 22 yards out. To start the fourth quarter, Saints kicker Charlie Durkee added three points from 32 yards out to give Atlanta only a 21–20 advantage. After 17 unanswered points from the Saints, Falcons kicker Wade Traynham ended Atlanta's scoring drought with a 26-yard field goal to lengthen the team's lead to 24–20. But it wouldn't be enough as the Saints scored the game's last points with a touchdown pass from quarterback Billy Kilmer to Kramer. New Orleans won the first Dixie Championship 27–24.

Atlanta didn't forget the bitter taste of the loss, reeling off wins in the rivalry's next nine games. In fact, Atlanta's defense kept New Orleans from scoring more than 20 points in each of those nine victories.

But New Orleans got itself back in the win column in 1974, defeating the Falcons in both meetings that season. Atlanta and New Orleans split the season series in each of the 1975, 1976, and 1977 seasons, adding to a spirited debate as to which team was better in this then-young rivalry.

The 1978 meetings may have been the ones that truly put this rivalry on the map in a national context. Both games bookended three consecutive NFL Sundays. In the first meeting on November 12, 1978, the Falcons traveled to New Orleans to renew the annual series and got out to a slow start. The Saints jumped on Atlanta early, rushing to a 17–3 halftime lead. With 2:23 remaining in the fourth quarter, the Falcons trailed 17–6 with the ball on their own 20-yard line. But Falcons quarterback and Ring of Honor member Steve Bartkowski drove down the field in 12 plays, which was capped off with running back Haskel Stanback bulldozing his way in for a one-yard touchdown to trim the Saints' lead to 17–13.

Still, this was New Orleans' game to lose, considering there were only 59 seconds remaining in the contest. Atlanta attempted an onside kick and failed to recover. The Saints ran three consecutive plays for eight yards. But Atlanta was able to stop the clock with timeouts to prevent the game from ending. New Orleans elected to gamble and went for it on fourth-and-two. But Falcons defensive lineman Jeff Yeates made perhaps the second-biggest play of the game for Atlanta by stuffing Saints running back Chuck Muncie for no gain. Atlanta took over possession of the ball, with the biggest play of the game coming next.

With 19 seconds remaining in the game and at the Atlanta 43-yard line, Bartkowski and the Falcons decided to take a shot downfield. Bartkowski revved his arm back and lofted a high, arching pass to the end zone, intended for receiver Wallace Francis. Saints defenders surrounded him but only managed to tip the ball into the air. The ball then landed, 57 yards later, in the hands of Falcons receiver Alfred Jackson for the game-winning score. The play was known as "Big Ben Right"—"Big Ben" being the Falcons' terminology for Hail Mary. It was also considered the first Big Ben play called in Falcons history. For Jackson, it was his only catch of the game. The Falcons won 20–17.

Two weeks later on November 26, the Falcons and Saints met again in Atlanta. Once again, the Saints held the advantage after three quarters, this time it being 17–10. But the Falcons scored 10 fourth-quarter points, ending with a one-yard Bartkowski touchdown toss to tight end Jim Mitchell to defeat the Saints by the same score of 20–17.

From 1980 to 1982 the Saints had some dreadful games against Atlanta, with the Falcons winning five straight in blowout fashion. But after defeating the Saints 35–0 in December of the 1982 season, New Orleans exacted revenge in the season finale with a 35–6 blowout win of its own.

Though the Falcons and Saints have played some important games in the late 2000s, the wild-card-round postseason matchup between the two teams in 1991 might rank as the most important game in the history of this rivalry—at least from the Falcons' perspective. It's the only time the two teams have met in the NFL playoffs, and it certainly wasn't free of drama. The Saints, who had earned wild-card berths in 1987 and 1990, broke through and won their first NFC West title during the regular season. But division foe Atlanta was waiting in the opening round. Atlanta was in its second season under former coach Jerry Glanville and finished 10–6 in the regular season. Rapper MC Hammer, at the height of his popularity, frequently appeared on the Falcons sideline during the season.

New Orleans held a 13–10 halftime lead with Saints kicker Morten Andersen making a 35-yard field goal to break a 10–10 tie late in the second quarter. Atlanta scored the only points of the third quarter, with quarterback Chris Miller finding receiver Michael Haynes in the right corner of the end zone for a touchdown. The Saints then methodically began a 19-play drive that ended with running back Dalton Hilliard scoring a touchdown from the 1-yard line. The Saints went back up 20–17 with the majority of the fourth quarter left to be played.

Falcons kicker Norm Johnson tied the game halfway through the game's final period with a 36-yard field goal. Johnson actually had a chance to give Atlanta a lead with a 54-yard attempt on Atlanta's next possession but had it blocked. Atlanta's defense, though, rose to the occasion and forced New Orleans to punt following the blocked field goal and with 4:34 remaining.

Atlanta moved the ball to its own 39-yard line before Miller threw a hitch to Haynes. Once Haynes caught the ball, he juked cornerback Milton Mack and bolted past the Saints secondary 61 yards for a touchdown, putting Atlanta up 27–20. The Saints threatened on the following drive but fell short. Quarterback Bobby Hebert lofted a pass down the sideline that was intercepted by Falcons cornerback Tim McKyer. McKyer lateraled the ball to corner Deion Sanders, who pitched it to safety Joe Fishback, who appeared to score another touchdown. Sanders' pitch was ruled a forward lateral by officials, so the touchdown was nullified. But it didn't matter, as the Falcons still came away with a victory over its bitter rival on the road in the playoffs.

While the playoff game is certainly Atlanta's most important win over New Orleans, the 2006 meeting in the Louisiana Superdome might hold that recognition for the Saints. On August 29, 2005, Hurricane Katrina hit the city of New Orleans, devastating much of the city's infrastructure. Strong winds and water damage resulted in $140 million worth of damages to the Louisiana Superdome, including holes ripped in the roof.

It took more than a year to repair the Saints' home, as the team split home games in 2005 between the Alamodome in San Antonio and Tiger Stadium at LSU. The Saints were also forced to play a home game against the Giants at the Meadowlands. New Orleans finished the season 3–13 and fired coach Jim Haslett.

Taking what was considered a risk at the time, the Saints signed former Chargers quarterback Drew Brees, who was coming off of shoulder surgery heading into the 2006 season. They also hired Sean Payton, previously assistant head coach and quarterbacks coach with Dallas, as the team's head coach.

New Orleans opened 2006 with two wins on the road, defeating Cleveland 19–14 and Green Bay 34–27. Atlanta was also 2–0, having defeated Carolina and Tampa Bay. The stage was set for a *Monday Night Football* showdown between the Falcons and Saints inside the Louisiana Superdome for the first time since the devastation of Hurricane Katrina.

From the first snap it was clear it would be New Orleans' night. Atlanta went three-and-out on its first series and was forced to punt. Safety Steve Gleason broke through the line and blocked Michael Koenen's punt, which was returned for a touchdown by Curtis Deloatch.

Morten Andersen—the former Saint—kicked a 26-yard field goal, though New Orleans remained ahead 7–3. After trading a series each, New Orleans scored another touchdown on an 11-yard double-reverse handoff to wideout Devery Henderson. The Saints never looked back, rolling to a 23–3 win in their repaired home.

The Falcons love to hate the Saints, and vice versa. But still, there's a feeling this game doesn't get the respect it deserves on a national level.

"This is one of the most overlooked rivalries in football right now," said Falcons running back Michael Turner.

Arthur Blank: The Owner Who Keeps On Giving

You can talk to him about the Falcons; send him a letter. He's visible. Sure, he has security, a retired FBI man. He has a driver, a retired state trooper. But he's visible and accessible.

Just think about the major complaint you hear about ownership of other professional teams in Atlanta. The Braves have a faceless owner. He is nameless too. His company, housed in a palace in Denver, I think, is a ghost to fans. It just came to me... Malone. The guy's name is Malone, and he owns a lot of land too.

What about the other owner(s)? Well, the Atlanta Spirit bungled away a hockey team. They bungled a sale of the Hawks. They were embroiled in a lawsuit...with one of their partners. They were invisible, except in the courtroom. Seven guys, or is it eight? Their owners would scurry away from media at hockey games.

One guy, Arthur Blank, is the majority owner of the Falcons, and you know he owns the Falcons. He does not scurry away. He brought stability to a franchise that had wobbled from 1966 to 2002.

We see him on the sideline, and we know somebody is in charge of the Falcons in case an iceberg looms. Michael Vick was an iceberg. The team hit it, sunk, and rose again with a coach who might be the best coach the team has ever had. That coach, Mike Smith, was hired by the GM, Thomas Dimitroff, who was hired by Blank and Rich McKay, the team president. The damage from Vick was repaired, and the Falcons became even stronger.

The Falcons have not been to the Super Bowl under Arthur Blank, but they are getting close. The one thing they did accomplish was slinging that anchor off their backs. You know the one: no back-to-back winning seasons…ever.

The Falcons went 11–5 in 2008 and 9–7 in 2009. Just for good measure, the Falcons went 13–3 in 2010.

Blank gave the Falcons a spanking-new facility in Flowery Branch, a comfortable place to practice and work. It is an attraction for free agents and coaches. He built dorms for the players to use during training camp. There were no more rental fees on the road for July workouts in the South Carolina swelter.

Blank does not give with one hand; he gives with two—one for the team, one for the city. But he did not suddenly get a conscience when he became more visible as owner of the Falcons and you could hear him on radio and see him on TV. Blank is the cofounder of the Home Depot, and before he retired in 2001, the company had donated more than $113 million to communities.

The Atlanta Falcons Youth Foundation is the largest owner-funded foundation in the NFL. Since 2002 the foundation has awarded more than $18 million in grants to more than 800 non-profit organizations. It wasn't about writing checks; it was about getting kids moving again. Georgia is one of the worst states in the U.S. for childhood obesity, and the foundation has sparked more than 10,000 kids per year to do more than 1 million hours of physical activity.

The well-heeled go to Falcons games, but the team takes some of that money and redirects it to the underserved. The initiatives include health and fitness, breast cancer awareness, combating hunger, the development of youth football, and other topics of outreach in underserved communities.

There is no blank check. That is, a check for thousands of dollars is not merely handed out, and that is the last the Falcons are heard from. A check for thousands was written for playground equipment in Vine City Park near the Georgia Dome, but on All Associates Day, where employees from various Blank endeavors

Falcons Records vs. the NFL

Against their rivals from the NFC South, the Atlanta Falcons have an overall winning record of 85–71. Surprisingly, it isn't the currently tough New Orleans Saints that have given Atlanta fits through the years; it's the Tampa Bay Buccaneers. The Falcons have a winning record against the Panthers and Saints, but a less-than-.500 record against the Buccaneers.

Atlanta's best overall win percentage is against the Chargers. Atlanta is 7–1 (.875) lifetime against San Diego.

The team that has given Atlanta the biggest fits throughout the years is Indianapolis. Atlanta has a 2–13 (.133) record against the Colts.

The Complete Breakdown

Opponent	W	L	T	W-L%
San Diego Chargers	7	1	0	0.875
Carolina Panthers	22	12	0	0.647
Buffalo Bills	6	4	0	0.600
New York Jets	6	4	0	0.600
New Orleans Saints	45	40	0	0.529
Baltimore Ravens	2	2	0	0.500
New England Patriots	6	6	0	0.500
New York Giants	10	10	0	0.500
Tampa Bay Buccaneers	18	19	0	0.486
Chicago Bears	12	13	0	0.480
Green Bay Packers	12	13	0	0.480
Tennessee Titans	6	7	0	0.462
Arizona Cardinals	11	14	0	0.440
Philadelphia Eagles	11	15	1	0.426
Cincinnati Bengals	5	7	0	0.417
Oakland Raiders	5	7	0	0.417
Jacksonville Jaguars	2	3	0	0.400
Minnesota Vikings	10	15	0	0.400
San Francisco 49ers	29	44	1	0.399
Seattle Seahawks	5	8	0	0.385
Dallas Cowboys	8	14	0	0.364
Miami Dolphins	4	7	0	0.364
St. Louis Rams	26	47	2	0.360
Denver Broncos	4	8	0	0.333
Houston Texans	1	2	0	0.333
Detroit Lions	11	23	0	0.324
Washington Redskins	6	14	1	0.310
Kansas City Chiefs	2	5	0	0.286
Cleveland Browns	3	10	0	0.231
Pittsburgh Steelers	2	12	1	0.167
Indianapolis Colts	2	13	0	0.133

come together, it was 180 associates who fixed up the park as well as a section of the Atlanta BeltLine at Washington Park.

In the last 10 years, associates at all of Blank's businesses have raised more than $4 million for more than 600 charitable organizations. The Arthur M. Blank Family Foundation has committed more than $250 million to nonprofit organizations.

He's a Yankee, but that's OK. Blank was born in Flushing, New York, and went to high school in Manhattan and college in Massachusetts. He cofounded the Home Depot in 1978, which is one of *Fortune* magazine's "Global Most Admired Companies."

There are some things to be upset with Blank about. He wants a new stadium, and he wants a lot of taxpayer money to help him build it, even if it means letting the Georgia Dome fall into disrepair. There is not enough hotel/motel tax money to give to the Falcons and keep the Georgia Dome viable for the Final Four and other mega-events. Most every owner in the NFL is like that, though. It is the fault of the politicians if they give an NFL owner money for a new stadium; it is not the owners' fault for asking.

The other issues? He enabled Michael Vick. The Falcons allowed Vick to be a prima donna and have his own security and curtail media access.

But the column filled with goodwill far outweighs the few demerits. Those who root for the Falcons will take an owner who has made far fewer mistakes than a lot of other owners, which includes those in Atlanta and around all of professional sports.

9 Remember Dan Reeves

Same guy on Monday that he was on Sunday. Same game on Tuesday that he was on Monday. There is a value in the steadiness of a head coach.

The Falcons were a steady team in 1998, which is why they were steady winners, clicking off 14 wins that season. That was preposterous for an Atlanta team 14 years ago. It is the only team in franchise history that made it to the Super Bowl, in what is still regarded as the most successful season in the history of the Falcons.

Reeves had the rudder, at least most of the way. He was direct with players and always seemed to be in command of the practice and the meeting rooms. That Falcons team resembled the Mike Smith teams in that Atlanta preferred to run the ball and then use the play-action pass.

When Reeves didn't have the rudder, there was a reason: he was in the hospital. He underwent heart surgery in the midst of the team's run to the Super Bowl. He came back in time to finish off the best season in the team's history, which included a 14–2 regular-season record and two playoff wins.

Reeves coached the Falcons from 1997 to 2003. He was fired while the team was headed toward a 5–11 season. This was nothing new: the star quarterback gets hurt, the season goes down the drain, and the coach is fired. Before there was doom for Jim Caldwell with the injury to Peyton Manning, there was doom for Reeves with the injury to Michael Vick.

The left-handed quarterback, the hub of everything the Falcons wanted to do on offense, broke his leg in the preseason, and Atlanta never found any traction. Some of that was Reeves' fault. He was

Dan Reeves: Coaching Highlights

Years as Falcons Head Coach: 7 (1997–2003)
Years as NFL Head Coach: 27 (1981–2003)
Falcons Record: 49–59–1 (.454)
NFL Record: 190–165–2 (.535)
Falcons Playoff Appearances: 2
NFL Playoff Appearances: 7
Falcons Division Championships: 1
NFL Division Championships: 6
Average Wins Per Season (Falcons): 7
Average Wins Per Season (NFL): 7.03
10+-Win Seasons (Falcons): 1
10+-Win Seasons (NFL): 9
Super Bowl Record (Falcons): 0–1
Super Bowl Record (NFL): 0–4

also in charge of player personnel and did not have a very effective backup, even as backups go.

Speaking about his ouster, Reeves said, "When Arthur told me he had made the decision about the end of the year, I knew it had to come to a fullness today. I'm an eternal optimist, so yeah, it was a surprise. But I'm also realistic enough about coaching to understand this is how it is in the NFL."

While Blank talked with reporters in one of the meeting rooms the day Reeves was fired, the coach was still in the building saying goodbye to his players, including Vick. There was supposed to be a rift between the coach and player during the season when Vick's rehabilitation dragged on, but it was not evident that last day.

"Dan is a sweet guy, very sweet," Vick said. "He's a guy that really cares about his players. I think he went the extra mile for us, and a lot of guys are going to miss him."

The Falcons were 3–10 when Reeves was fired. Ironically, the dismissal came right after Vick returned to the lineup and led the team to an overtime win over Carolina. It was that kind of upside-down season. Reeves began the season with his 199th career victory, a 27–13 win at Dallas, the team he played for as a pro. Was it a good omen, a sign the Falcons might survive without Vick? Not really. Atlanta went on to lose seven in a row.

Reeves finally got his 200th win at New York against the Giants on November 9, one of the teams where he had been head coach.

Reeves finished with a career record of 201–174–2, including the playoffs. When he was fired by the Falcons in 2003, there were only five NFL coaches who had won more games, and it was an impressive list: Don Shula, George Halas, Tom Landry, Curly Lambeau, and Chuck Noll. He guided the Broncos to three AFC championships and the Falcons to an NFC title.

10 Mike Smith Is Solid

Several months after the Baltimore Ravens won the Super Bowl to cap the 2000 season, a contingent of Ravens went on a football mission trip to Mexico. There was a start-up youth league on the outskirts of Cancun.

On the first day of the camp, the defensive line coach of the Ravens, Mike Smith, was on his knees holding a tackling dummy for a kid who might have been eight years old. Imagine that. Mike Smith, a professional football coach, was coaching a kid who might have as much chance of flying to the moon as he would of playing in the NFL.

"That's who he is," said Phil Savage, who was the player personnel director for the Ravens at the time and later the general manager of the Cleveland Browns. "Mike is salt of the earth. I don't know if I have heard anybody say a negative thing about Mike Smith."

Mike Smith: Coaching Highlights

Years as Falcons Head Coach: 4 (2008–11)
Years as NFL Head Coach: 4 (2008–11)
Years Coaching in NFL: 13 (1999–2011—nine as assistant or coordinator, four as head coach)
Falcons Record: 43–21 (.672)
NFL Record: 43–21 (.672)
Falcons Playoff Appearances: 3
NFL Playoff Appearances: 3
Division Championships: 1
Average Wins Per Season (Falcons): 10.75
10+-Win Seasons (Falcons): 3

That is an unusual thing in a competitive business like the NFL. You always hear something crappy about a guy on another team. It's that old saying in reverse: "What goes around, comes around." Mike Smith never starts anything that will go around coaching circles.

In his first four years as Falcons head coach, Smith is 43–24, including playoffs. The Falcons, who went 43 years without back-to-back winning seasons, have had four consecutive winning seasons under Smith. His .672 regular-season winning percentage is the highest for any coach in franchise history.

Smith has friends on every rung of the NFL ladder. He stayed at Tennessee Tech so long (1987–98) that assistant coaches came and went and came and went. They spread out all over football.

Why Tech for so long? A native of Daytona Beach, Florida, he went to East Tennessee State and had some regional ties, but that might not explain everything. It could have been a lack of ambition to climb over people to get a better job. It could have been he was happy being a position coach and trying to perfect his craft. Maybe Mike Smith didn't know how good a coach Mike Smith was.

It seems perplexing. Smith was at Tennessee Tech for 12 seasons. Have you been to Cookeville? Not a lot going on there.

The students who go there call it "Cook-Vegas." Smith was defensive line coach, then special teams coordinator, then defensive coordinator. He went to the Ravens in 1999. And off he went; his career bloomed. Smith was with the Ravens four years and then was named defensive coordinator of the Jacksonville Jaguars in 2003.

Smith is a gentleman, but there is an intensity to him too. When William Moore, the gifted second-year safety, botched a coverage in a 2010 practice, Smith steamed over to Moore on the practice field. Smith screamed at Moore—not for the blown play but for what led to it, which was being late for meetings and not paying attention in film study.

Smith pays attention. It can be a training-camp workout in the August swelter or a midweek practice getting prepared to play a downtrodden opponent, but it's all important to him.

It's interesting that Smith and former Ravens coach Brian Billick married sisters. The two coaches couldn't be more different. Billick was a guy who was OK with being plastered on every billboard in town; Smith settled for a page in the media guide.

You think Mike Smith can coach? Wait until you see him in the film room studying players and giving his two cents. "If he ever leaves coaching," said one former NFL general manager, "there should be teams lining up to make him their director of scouting. He knows players."

When Mike Smith gets fired by the Falcons—and they all get fired—he will thank everybody in the building for the opportunity. He will go out the front door. It would not be surprising if he doesn't have a farewell press conference. Some coaches have one; some don't.

One thing is certain: Smith put some consistency into the Falcons on the field. And for that, the franchise is lucky to have him.

11 Neon Deion

Deion Sanders' alter ego, "Prime Time," had the do-rag going out of the back of the helmet. He had the strut to the end zone and all the other circus acts. He was the godfather of the end-zone fun that filled television screens on Sundays.

But he was much more than a sideshow. He had closing speed and instincts. The theatrics distracted from it, but you could see how Sanders really could shut down one side of the field. If he got his hands on the ball, there was always a chance for a touchdown, because he was not only fast but just impossible to get a clear shot at when he was running with the ball.

Think about that talent. He held out in 1989, but when he got on the field for the first time that year, he returned a punt 68 yards for a touchdown. He returned six for touchdowns in his career.

Sure, there were some issues with tackling and run support, but as the NFL became more quarterback-centric in the late 1990s, Sanders had value. He had so much value that after five years with the Falcons and one year with the 49ers, the Dallas Cowboys made him the highest-paid defensive player in the NFL.

No question, Sanders could run. The thing that made him fascinating was that he could run in two sports—baseball and football. He was the first athlete to score an NFL touchdown and hit a home run in the same week.

On October 10, 1992, Sanders was in uniform for the Braves. That was a Saturday. The next day, on Sunday, he was in uniform for the Falcons playing the Dolphins in Miami. He hopped a plane from Miami and was back in Atlanta for another postseason baseball game that night.

It was a circus act, and Braves manager Bobby Cox was not especially amused. Sanders got back to Atlanta, but Cox was not going to play Sanders and give him the benefit of being the only professional athlete to play a game in two sports in the same day. Cox was not a fan of Deion's alter ego, Prime Time.

Still, Sanders is the only player to get in both a World Series and a Super Bowl. How many players can score five different ways: kickoff return, punt return, fumble return, interception return, and receiving? There are guys who might think they can do it, but only one has done it in the NFL.

Sanders went to eight Pro Bowls, but more than anything, he established the shutdown corner as a glamour position. He was named first-team All-Pro nine times, and he revolutionized the position—not by being the only cornerback in the game who could shut down one side of the field, but by illuminating the position.

Sanders led the NFL in kickoff-return yardage one season (1992) and punt-return average another season (1998). He had 19 career touchdowns off interceptions and returns, an NFL record. Sanders had 53 career interceptions with the Falcons, 49ers, Cowboys, Redskins, and Ravens. He was a member of the NFL's All-Decade Team of the 1990s as both a cornerback and a punt returner.

Sanders retired from professional football in 2001, only to be lured back by the Ravens in 2004. He retired for good early in 2006 and is now an analyst for the NFL Network. He was inducted into the Pro Football Hall of Fame on August 6, 2011.

12 The Big Heart of Warrick Dunn

Warrick Dunn's mother, Betty Smothers, a police officer in Baton Rouge, Louisiana, was shot to death in a robbery while escorting a grocery store manager to a night-deposit drop at a bank in her off-duty job as a security guard.

When he got the news, he lay in bed in his dorm at Florida State and cried. Dunn said she was his best friend. His roommate, the quarterback Charlie Ward, could not comfort him.

"I don't even know how I played football," said Dunn, who played for the Falcons from 2002 to 2007. "That stuff can take over your mind and break you down. It was such a struggle, and Charlie would have to listen to me just cry in our room."

Dunn said it took years for him to deal with the murder of his mother, who was killed in January 1993, two days after his 18th birthday. He became the surrogate parent to five younger brothers and sisters with help from his maternal grandmother, Willie Wheeler.

"When your rock is taken away from you, you have to rebuild yourself," Dunn said. "Eventually you have to move on. You have to have a life. You have to be happy. You have to be complete again. I'll never be complete, but I'm happy."

Dunn was considered too small to be the featured running back, at 5'9" and 180 pounds. It was the mark against him at Tampa Bay with the Bucs and in Atlanta. But in the NFL playoffs for the 2004 season, in January 2005, Dunn crushed the St. Louis Rams for 142 yards and two touchdowns for the Falcons. He had touchdown runs of 62 and 19 yards in the 47–17 victory.

"He is so elusive, man. When he gets in that hole it's hard for anyone to get a clean shot at him," center Todd McClure said.

"He knows how to duck and hit the creases. Guys square up and think they are going to make the tackle, but they have no chance."

Dunn ran for 1,106 yards in the regular season. It was the payoff for the Falcons, who gave Dunn a $6.5 million signing bonus in 2002. He wasn't too small. He wasn't just a situational back that was supposed to play just on third down.

"I think I've had to prove a lot of things, and that's always given me my drive," Dunn said. "I know people looked at my size and said, 'He can't do this every down.'"

Dunn played five seasons in Tampa Bay and became a free agent following the 2001 season.

Warrick Dunn signs autographs for a group of kids after Falcons practice in Flowery Branch on July 31, 2007.

It was Arthur Blank, the Falcons owner, who wanted high-character guys, and he told the personnel people to close the deal on Dunn.

Blank, like a lot of people, was impressed by Dunn's record of community service, particularly a program called Homes for the Holidays, which Dunn started in 1997 while he was with the Bucs. In that program, Dunn makes a down payment of $5,000 on a new house for a single mother and works with local businesses to furnish the home.

Dunn started the program because his mother never realized her dream of owning a home.

Dunn was just 23 and in his second season in the NFL when he brought his siblings—who were 17, 16, and 15—to live with him in Tampa. While his teammates went out on the town, Dunn went home to help with schoolwork.

"It's forced me not to want to have kids," Dunn said, before breaking into a wide smile. "I gave up a lot of things I wanted to do, so now I'm getting some of the partying things out of my system so I can settle down."

It is difficult to extract Dunn's story from him. When he speaks it is barely above a whisper. He is off-the-charts modest. His car in 2006 is an example. In a parking lot full of SUVs and chrome, Dunn flipped a playbook into a 1993 Mitsubishi Galant with 132,000 miles. It was his car in high school and college.

"Sweet, isn't it?" Dunn said.

He had nice cars, but he wanted to save the miles, not show off. The Galant was the grocery-getter, the car that took him 44 miles every day from home near downtown to the Falcons' facility in Flowery Branch.

Four years after the conclusion of his 12-year career, Dunn still manages the Warrick Dunn Family Foundation. He is still seeding homes for the underserved in communities in Florida, Atlanta, and Baton Rouge.

Dunn rushed for 10,967 yards in his career. He caught 510 passes for 4,339 yards. He was productive on the field, to be sure, but one of the 100 things in this book has to be his production off the field. Thank Warrick Dunn for that before you thank him for the yards and highlights.

13 Arch and Wes

I get tired of Howie and JB and the other talking hairdos, trying to outdo one another. I can take only so much of the two-faced Mike Strahan calling players quitters. Collinsworth is pretty good, but you don't get him Sunday at 1:00.

You can give me Wes and Arch at 1:00. I'll take them any Sunday.

Do yourself a favor, if you haven't already. Get a radio and put it in the garage. Get another radio and put it on the screened-in porch. Now putz around for three hours. Rake leaves, wash the car, clean the garage, fix the bike, cut the wood. Just keep the radio turned up for Wes Durham and Dave Archer, and you will get *X*s and *O*s and some passion for Falcons football and the NFL.

The radio voices of the Falcons make the game sing on Sunday afternoons. Even when I'm in the press box at the Falcons covering the game in person, I listen to these guys on headphones. I jumped on MARTA one Sunday in 2011, went four stops before I realized I left my headphones at home on the treadmill, hopped off at Inman Park, and went back and got them. I just made it for kickoff.

Archer sees things—the coverage, the breakdown in protection, the misread by the quarterback, the wrong cut by the back, the missed block on the backside. Most of us have to lock on to the line to see the wrong step. Archer sees the wrong step by the lineman but also sees the path of the ball. Really. It's like film study some Sundays.

That's why I listen. I have my eye on one thing; Archer has his eye on something more important.

Throughout the fall of 2011, Archer would bemoan the lack of a screen game by the Falcons. When Atlanta hired Dirk Koetter from the Jaguars, you know what his mandate was? Develop a screen game. The Falcons never used running back Jacquizz Rodgers as effectively as the Saints used Darren Sproles in the screen game.

Archer is not a house man for the Falcons. He will question execution and performance. He does not lay waste to the Falcons like a columnist, of course, but he will hold a player accountable. That makes the listener trust him. If Archer can zing the Falcons for a bad play, you can trust him when he extols a good one.

I have heard that somebody in the Falcons brass will grumble from time to time about some Arch calls. He still has his job, though. He was a quarterback for the Falcons from 1984 to 1987. He has an understanding of the game and puts it on the plate for listeners in digestible chunks…and with a little wit, humor, and bite.

Durham, meanwhile, is all over the dial. He does the Falcons. He does Georgia Tech. He does talk radio. He is FM and AM. Wes has a big voice, and it's obvious it's him when it blares through the speaker.

A lot of us were worried he might head back to North Carolina once his dad, the legendary voice of the Tar Heels, retired. But Wes said he was staying, and he stayed.

Durham is perfect for the effervescent Mike Smith, who can stomp along the sideline and get wiggy with referees. Durham seems to notice Smith before the rest of us in the press box. "And look at Mike Smith!" he will exclaim. A lot of Wes' stuff should come with an exclamation point. He's into it.

Archer knows the rules, and heaven help the referee who doesn't or who has to think about a call or ask for help. "C'mon fellas," Archer will say into the mic. He will plead for them to make a decision without having a huddle.

When Pete Van Wieren went to the house and retired, I needed a crew to admire and call No. 1. The Braves have some professionals, and I will get accustomed to them—you know what they say about following legends. Steve Holman of the Hawks is a way of life around here. But for now Wes and Arch are kingpins, at least in my garage and on my screened-in porch.

14 The Big Back of Gerald Riggs

You know how they talk about how the game has evolved, how the players are bigger and faster and capable of running you over? You know how they talk about the size of backs and all that blather? It makes it sound as if the guys who played 20 years ago were as big as peanuts.

So I invite you to walk up to Gerald Riggs and tell me this guy wasn't a load to bring down.

Before there was the big back Michael Turner, there was the big back Gerald Riggs. All those records Turner is assaulting now belong or belonged to Riggs. He was 6'2" and 240 pounds, which makes him taller and just seven pounds lighter than Turner.

Riggs was a fullback coming out of Arizona State, so he was not a feature runner in college but a blocker and pass catcher. When he got to the NFL Combine, which was in its first year, Riggs ran some sprints and turned some heads.

"Not many scouts realized how fast I was for my size," Riggs said. "I could be explosive."

The Falcons figured out pretty quickly in the NFL Combine just how good Riggs could be. They picked him up in the first round, ninth overall in the 1982 draft. The Falcons draft picks did not always turn out so well, but this one did.

Riggs, who made the Pro Bowl three times, is the Falcons' all-time leading rusher, with 6,631 yards in his career. He carried the ball 1,587 yards in his career with Atlanta, which lasted from 1982 through 1988.

In 1985 he rushed for 1,719 yards and caught 33 passes for 267 yards and scored 10 touchdowns.

Riggs' best game with the Falcons came on November 2, 1984, when he went for 202 yards against the Saints. But it wasn't just his running with the ball that made him a superb player. It was his pass catching. He finished his NFL career with 201 receptions for 1,516 yards.

"I just had a natural ability to catch the ball because of playing basketball in high school," Riggs said. "I was a fairly good route runner. [I] had a favorite route...called 'scram,' which usually required a smaller, shifty back running a post out of the back-field.... The only thing about all the passes I caught: I never caught a touchdown pass."

Riggs' other regret is that he wanted to play in the same back-field with William Andrews, a massive fullback. Andrews and Riggs shared carries in 1982 and 1983, but there was never a commitment to use them at the same time.

"We would have terrorized the league," Riggs said. "It never materialized due to William getting hurt. He was a great football player."

Riggs said it is still a mystery to him how the Falcons struggled season after season. The drafts seemed to produce good talent, but there was always a missing piece.

"There were good football minds there," Riggs said. "People like Eddie LeBaron and Tom Braatz. Football is a matter of chemistry, and sometimes we didn't have it. Things just never got pulled together. When Taylor [Smith] started to run the team, it was going in the right direction."

One of Riggs' favorite quarterbacks was Dave Archer, the current color analyst for the Falcons. Archer was always looking out for Riggs and the Falcons' best opportunity to move the ball and would let the offense know in the huddle to "check with me" at the line.

"Dave could read a defense, and if they were geared up for the pass, he would check to run," Riggs said. "When the defense was geared to run, he still wouldn't let them dictate to us what we were going to call, so we [would] run it anyway. We didn't feel like defenses could dictate to us to get us out of the run."

The end in Atlanta for Riggs came before the 1989 season. He was watching the draft and wondering who the Falcons might select. Then he started hearing the chatter on the television that the Falcons might swing a trade for the new regime of Marion Campbell.

"I never saw it coming," Riggs said. "Never knew it was going to happen. There was one minute left on the clock before the Falcons' pick, and then I got a call from Marion, and he said, 'Gerald, we're going to trade you.' That was that. 'We wish you well. Goodbye.'"

Riggs went to Washington, which was not a surprise. The previous season, the Redskins' general manager Bobby Beathard had stopped Riggs after a game at Atlanta–Fulton County Stadium. "We'd love to get you in Washington next season," Beathard had told Riggs.

"I shrugged it off," Riggs said. "The next season I was in Washington."

Riggs started well with the Redskins, with 400 yards rushing early in the season. But when he hurt his foot, he was sidelined, and the Redskins were not anxious to put him back in the lineup. Riggs played for the Redskins for three seasons before retiring. He lives in Chattanooga, Tennessee.

15 The Wonder of Vick

On Sunday, November, 10, 2002, Michael Vick served up his specialty of running and eluding and keeping plays alive. The Falcons trailed the Steelers in the fourth quarter by 17 points, and Vick made a tie seem like a win.

There was 12:58 to play when the Falcons scored two touchdowns and added a field goal on three possessions to tie the game and send it to overtime. Mr. Improv scored with 42 seconds left, darting through the Steelers defense for the tying score on a mushy field that should have ruined a running quarterback.

"If you don't enjoy watching him play, there's something wrong with you," Falcons coach Dan Reeves said. "He's special.

"Our guys had the feeling that, if we just kept working, we've got a quarterback who can win for us. When the game's on the line, he wants it. I'm just sorry we didn't win it in overtime because I really thought we had a chance."

The Steelers got after Vick with a spy, a player devoted to corking Vick's big runs. The mean-spirited Joey Porter hit Vick on the first series and forced a fumble. Vick kept playing. Porter hit Vick, knocked him down, laid on top of him.

"He's more relaxed than what I thought he was going to be," Porter said. "Everybody was telling us that he was going to run here and run there. He dropped back and threw the ball. He wasn't really worried about the pressure."

Mike and the Moped

I was driving to the Falcons training camp at Furman in 2002, and the story was already making its way down the highway and into living rooms and into lore: Michael Vick threw a pass so hard it busted up a motorbike.

It wasn't like he stood 20 feet away and cracked that fender like an egg. Vick was 40 yards away. He zinged a pass with that sensational arm. It kept going and going, and then...*crack!*

"He [Vick] overthrows a receiver, and look what the ball did to my scooter here," said Falcons defensive back Ashley Ambrose, pointing to the metal fender. It now has a crack and a hole, courtesy of the Vick pass that traveled 40 yards before hammering the scooter that was parked in the back of the end zone.

There were all kinds of wow moments with Vick that August.

Wide receiver Shawn Jefferson watched Vick roll out in one of the first practices of camp. The quarterback delivered a pass that Jefferson, a 10-year veteran, says he had never seen in the NFL. "On the run," Jefferson said, "he throws the ball 65 yards. On the run!"

"Give Mike credit," said Atlanta wide receiver Brian Finneran. "He took some big hits and got through the adversity. That's what he does."

Vick completed 24 of 46 passes for 294 yards in what ended as a tie with the Steelers. He still managed 38 yards on 10 attempts. The Falcons converted nine of 20 third-down plays. Vick converted two third-down plays when the Falcons had to get more than 20 yards for a first down.

"That was all Mike," Reeves said. "Believe me, there aren't a lot of plays you can call in that situation, but Mike gives you that chance. They did a good job catching us with some blitzes and sacking us, but Mike made some great throws."

The Falcons had started the season 1–3. The tie with the Steelers pushed them to 5–3–1, and they were on to the playoffs and more Vick magic.

16 Dave Hampton: 1,000 Yards...or Not

The game with the Kansas City Chiefs was stopped for Dave Hampton. There was applause. He had become the first 1,000-yard rusher in Falcons history. It was December 17, 1972, a day to remember for Hampton...or not.

When he carried the ball in the fourth quarter for one yard and reached the 1,000-yard milestone, it was all sweet. It was the last game of the regular season. But the Falcons had no luck back in those days. The team was still in its infancy, and good news was hard to come by.

Hampton got the ball again in that game, slipped on ice, and lost six yards. That put him at less than 1,000 yards, and when the Chiefs scored late to take a lead, the Falcons had to throw to try and win. Hampton never got a chance to get back to 1,000 yards. It was the milestone that never really happened. He finished the season with 995 yards.

"Right now, it's the most disappointing thing that has ever happened to me," Hampton said after the game.

The next year, in 1973, the Falcons had a pretty fair team, a squad that won seven in a row in one stretch. Hampton was the workhorse again and was once again chasing 1,000 yards.

Atlanta was playing the Saints at home during the last game of the season, on December 16. Hampton came into the game 87 yards short of 1,000. Surely he could get 87 yards against the lowly Saints.

Coach Norm Van Brocklin was determined to make it happen. The Dutchman kept calling plays for Hampton. Even while trying to protect a 14–10 lead, Van Brocklin called for Hampton to run the ball on fourth down. The Falcons were even within field-goal range, and Hampton still got the ball on a fourth-down play. But it wasn't enough. Hampton didn't make the yards he needed. He managed 997 yards for the season.

The chase for 1,000 yards looked over for Hampton. He was injured much of the 1974 season, but in 1975 he came back determined to have a finishing kick to his career. And he did. A coach went to the mat for Hampton again. This time it was Marion Campbell. The Falcons (4–9) were losing by nine to the Packers with just less than three minutes to play. Campbell was not going to throw long and throw long again and then hope to get an onside kick.

He told his offense to run the ball with Hampton. Campbell put the former Heisman Trophy winner Pat Sullivan (Auburn) into the game as quarterback, with instructions for the line to block for Hampton, one of the team's most popular players. He needed 28 yards.

Hampton got 30. One play went for 22 yards, and the Green Bay crowd, assured their team was going to win anyway, cheered and cheered for Hampton when he got four yards on his final carry of 1975. He got a standing ovation and then came out of the game. Hampton was not going to be denied again with a last-second slip.

He finished the season with 1,002 yards. The chase was over.

Hampton finished his career with the Eagles in 1976 and ended up averaging 4.0 yards per carry, which is a nice benchmark for any running back.

17 The New Stadium

It's coming. It will probably look like a spaceship, all glass and polished steel on the outside. It will be visible on the flight into

Hartsfield but perhaps not as visible as the white, marshmallowy roof of the Dome.

The Falcons will have a new stadium in five years, maybe sooner. Arthur Blank, the owner, will pay for half of it, and the taxpayers will pay for the other half. If the taxpayers were really upset, they would light torches and form a mob down at the gold dome of the capitol and arrest the politicians. If the ticket holders cared enough, they would brace themselves for what comes next: personal seat licenses. To buy tickets you have to be part of the PSL program, which adds to the ticket price.

The fact is, we love our NFL, and there will be no mob and no revolt. The stadium will get built, and Atlantans will take great joy in it. Arthur Blank has done his best to put a winning product on the field, and the fans and business leaders will back him 100 percent by backing this new stadium.

Blank is a nice-guy owner, as opposed to Al Davis, who was not a nice-guy owner and did not get a new stadium.

We want a Super Bowl too. That's part of the deal. It happened in Dallas, Detroit, and New York. If an owner, who shares revenue

What Happens at the Georgia Dome Besides Falcons Games

In addition to becoming the home of the Falcons, the Georgia Dome has hosted numerous events since it opened its doors. Various concerts (such as U2 and the Rolling Stones) and other sporting events (such as the SEC, ACC, and NCAA basketball tournaments and WWE wrestling shows) have made their way to the Georgia Dome throughout the years. Georgia State University's football team, which began play in 2010, plays its home games at the Georgia Dome. The Georgia Dome also hosted Super Bowl XXXIV, which turned out to be one of the better championship games ever played. The St. Louis Rams edged the Tennessee Titans 23–16, with Titans receiver Kevin Dyson's outstretched arm landing a yard short of the goal line on the game's final play.

with his business partners (the other owners), gets a new stadium built, he/she is rewarded with the Super Bowl.

Did you think it was all about the weather when the NFL refused to bring the Super Bowl here again? Atlanta was shaved off the list, supposedly, because of an ice storm at the last Super Bowl it hosted. My feeling is Atlanta was shaved off the list so it would get busy with plans for a new stadium.

I don't believe the financial hocus pocus the NFL puts out in regard to the economic impact of the Super Bowl. I think they are a bunch of liars when it comes to the exact figure. Still, the Super Bowl is a boon to the local economy. Some of the money is trucked out of town to the headquarters, for instance, of Hyatt and Marriott, but a lot of it does stay here. Good for us.

The Falcons' new stadium will be a grand place, and it will be designed to be loud. Seattle's outdoor stadium is loud, and I have a feeling the Falcons have been taking notes and want to make their outdoor stadium loud too.

The new stadium—which will be named Home Depot Park or UPS Stadium or Coca-Cola Stadium, or Chick-fil-A something or other—will be built up the hill on Northside Drive, up from the Dome.

One important thing to remember is the Dome might not be going anywhere. The place looks 10 years old on the outside. It hosts 200 events per year, which means there are 190 things going on that have nothing to do with the Falcons, who play eight home games and two preseason games there.

There are still negotiations under way to make sure the Dome gets its fair share of the hotel/motel tax money for upkeep. That ensures the SEC Championship Game stays there, along with the preseason Chick-fil-A game, the Chick-fil-A Bowl, the monster truck pulls, and all the other glorious events.

I'm not looking forward to the new stadium. The press box will likely be on the roof, halfway to the moon. Worse, it will be on the roof above an end zone. The media urchins will be the first to feel the sleet in the December games.

People ask me if I watch the game on television and then write my story. From where the Falcons will put me at the new stadium, I probably will have to watch it on TV.

18 Mike Turner: Swell Guy

I am going to scream out loud if one morning I pick up the paper and Michael Turner's mug shot is on the top of the sports page. I mean, I will throw that newspaper in the middle of the fireplace in August and strike a match.

Are you with me on this?

Turner is a hulk at 245 pounds. He runs over people. The guy really does block for himself. His kneepads hit the tackler first, and then the rest of Turner runs by or over the defender. Opponents know the best way to bring him down is never, ever letting him get going.

But Turner is also soft-spoken, a team-first guy. He has some fun when he lets the goatee grow a little bit. He stays in a corner locker across the aisle from the fun-and-gun wideouts. He doesn't complain about injuries.

So if he gets arrested, I won't handle it well. There are many more good guys in the NFL than bad guys. There are guys who make mistakes and guys who really make mistakes. Turner is not going to make a mistake. He is a good guy.

About the only time he stiff-armed me for an interview was before the playoff game with the Giants in January 2012. The trainer was standing over him with 10 minutes left in the interview time, and Turner was trying to rehab a groin injury. He had to go. Other than that, he is standing by his locker during the weekday interview times. Some players blow it off and hang out in the trainer's room, which is off limits to the media. Turner understands the responsibilities of being a team's feature back.

On the field, Turner was the only member of the Falcons offense to make ESPN's All–NFC South Team. The only year the Falcons have not made the playoffs since Turner has been here (2009), he missed five games with an injury.

He ran for 1,340 yards (4.5 average) in 2011, and the Falcons were in the playoffs. He went for 1,371 yards (4.1) in 2010, and the Falcons were in the playoffs. He went for 1,699 yards (4.5) in 2008, and the Falcons were in the playoffs.

The Falcons had a stretch play for Warrick Dunn—a fast, elusive back. They have the same play for Turner. Matt Ryan will hand it off, and Turner will go right, and the defense will get strung out, and then, just like that, Turner will make a cutback, get a block, and be to the second level of the defense where a linebacker will take him on. Turner can be tackled by one guy, but it is rare and usually early in the game. When it is late, and the legs of defenders are worn down, Turner will make the cut and plow through late-game arm tackles.

It is Turner—not quarterback Matt Ryan or wide receivers Roddy White and Julio Jones—who gives the Falcons their identity. Even when the Falcons drafted the home-run hitter Jones in 2011, they knew whom to build an offense around.

"To me that has been the most misrepresented statement about us, that we lost our identity," said Thomas Dimitroff, Atlanta's general manager, who signed Turner to a six-year contract in 2008. "I started hearing that earlier in the season. We never lost our identity. We are based around a strong running game.

"We have always talked about working down the middle of the field. When we acquired Julio, we never had plans to go away from having Michael run the rock."

When Turner went five consecutive games without a 100-yard game the second half of the 2011 season, the idea crept into place that he was wearing down and maybe the Falcons needed to become a more fanciful offense. Turner is 30 years old and spent four years in San Diego (2004–2007) as a backup to LaDainian Tomlinson. Punishing blows make a short shelf life for an NFL running back, and it was Turner's eighth season.

"I'm not wearing down," Turner said after the regular season. "We just lost some of our chemistry there for a few games. It fell off a little bit; hopefully we have our consistency back."

Ovie Mughelli, a Pro Bowl fullback in 2010, was placed on injured reserve October 25 with a knee injury, and the Falcons lost some traction in their run game. They seemed to coalesce and reconstitute the run game in the last regular-season game of 2011 against Tampa Bay when Turner ran for 172 yards, albeit against a team that lost its last 10 games of the season.

Turner still has something left. He is nearing the end of his deal with the Falcons, and the fifth season might be his last hurrah here, which is pretty good for a guy who invites contact. Here's what else is pretty good: no issues off the field. That is a big deal to the Falcons. They invested their money in a good running back and a good guy.

19 Riggs Enters Record Books As Falcons Top Rusher

Atlanta Falcons running back Gerald Riggs was already a force to be reckoned with. Since 1982 Riggs had been brutalizing tacklers and flummoxing defensive coordinators, but only as a starter since 1984.

That's what made Riggs such an astonishing runner. In just four short years Riggs rewrote the Atlanta record book. In his first two seasons, Riggs accumulated 736 yards as a backup running back. But over the next four seasons as a starter, he rushed for 5,407 yards— 1,486 in 1984, 1,719 in 1985, 1,327 in 1986, and 875 in 1987.

It was a game on December 6, 1987, in Dallas where Riggs got to etch his name into the record book as Atlanta's all-time leading rusher. Riggs passed William Andrews with a five-yard run in the third quarter of Atlanta's 21–10 victory in Dallas. Riggs carried the ball 30 times that Sunday for 119 yards, but even with the success of the day, both personally and as a team, Riggs was suffering from some tough times in Atlanta.

"You don't know what it's like when you are losing," Riggs told the Associated Press. "You don't know what it's like going in your own house and some people don't want to see you. It's been darn tough."

Riggs' 119 yards helped push the Falcons that day and stopped a six-game losing streak. His 6,024 career rushing yards were more than any Atlanta Falcon had ever gained.

Riggs played one more season in Atlanta, tacking on 607 more rushing yards to his record. He still sits in first place with 6,631 rushing yards for the Falcons. He's 645 yards ahead of the No. 2 rusher, William Andrews, and 1,350 yards ahead of the leading active rusher for the Falcons, Michael Turner.

Hometown Kid, Keith Brooking

Everyone loves a hometown hero. That's just the way things go in sports. If a player is a local guy or has even grown up in the same state as the pro team he plays for, naturally the fans are inclined to favor him. This was the case for Keith Brooking, a man who was born and raised in Georgia and ended up playing for the Atlanta Falcons.

Brooking was born on October 30, 1975, in Senoia, Georgia, a town roughly one hour away from Atlanta. He never ventured far from his hometown, playing high school, college, and pro football all within 40 miles of each other.

He attended East Coweta High School in Sharpsburg, Georgia, right down the road from his hometown. Most athletes who make it to the pros are naturally gifted in many ways early on, and it was no different in Brooking's case. While in high school he played tight end, defensive lineman, and linebacker for the ECHS Indians, making an impact wherever they put him on the field.

He could make big hits, play in coverage, get after opposing quarterbacks, and even catch touchdowns when needed. It was no wonder he became a highly coveted athlete by the end of his high school tenure. In his ECHS career he finished with 250 tackles, 53 receptions for 622 yards and seven touchdowns, and was a three-time varsity letterman. He also won the Indians' Scholar-Athlete Award, proving there was more to him than just athletic ability. It made sense that he wound up playing college ball at one of the brightest academic schools in the nation.

Brooking chose to stick nearby to his roots with his decision to attend Georgia Tech. Located in the heart of Atlanta, he made an even bigger name for himself in the state and also on a national level.

The first year he played for the Yellow Jackets was 1994. As a true freshman Brooking showed solid improvement throughout the year and eventually earned a few starts later on in the season, as Don Hickson dealt with some injury issues down the stretch. Brooking recorded a season-high 10 tackles against Wake Forest that year and looked like a promising young star for the Jackets going forward.

Everyone knew his potential, but no one quite expected the jump he would make between his freshman and sophomore campaigns. In 1995 Brooking led the ACC in tackles per game with 13.3. He finished the final nine games of the season with double-digit tackles in each and even recorded 20 tackles in two separate performances. It was a breakout year for the Georgian, and it only foreshadowed great things to come.

1996 was another impressive year, as Brooking was the Jackets' top defensive player and second-leading tackler in the ACC. He was always on the field, playing just about every down Tech needed him to.

He finished his senior year with 131 tackles in 1997, earned second-team All-ACC honors, and was well on his way to becoming a star at the next level. He finished college as Georgia Tech's all-time leading tackler. *Sports Illustrated* projected him as the No. 7 overall pick for the 1998 NFL Draft.

After spending his entire life in Georgia, would it have been fitting for him to play anywhere else but Atlanta in the NFL? Obviously not, as the Falcons selected Brooking with the No. 12 overall pick in 1998. He was already a fan favorite because he was from the area, and his play made it tough not to like him.

Brooking played 15 games in his rookie year with the Falcons, recording 26 tackles, two forced fumbles, and an interception. The Falcons saw more success than ever before in the history of their franchise in 1998, making it all the way to the Super Bowl. Atlanta had not made a Super Bowl appearance in 32 years of operation,

Keith Brooking drops back in pass coverage against the Denver Broncos in Denver on October 31, 2004. The Falcons defeated the Broncos 41–28.

so it was an epic moment for the franchise and its city. Maybe Brooking broke some sort of curse placed upon the Falcons in the past? It's doubtful, but his eight tackles in the NFC Championship Game surely helped fuel Atlanta to the promised land.

Even though the Falcons were defeated by John Elway and the Denver Broncos that season, Brooking immediately made the most of his NFL career. The following season he recorded 94 tackles in just 13 games played. It was becoming clear he was a force to be reckoned with at the highest level.

A season-ending foot injury caused Brooking to miss a large part of the 2000 campaign. It didn't seem to linger too long into the subsequent season, though, as he blew everyone out of the water in 2001, finishing with 167 tackles and making his first-ever Pro Bowl. The retirement of Falcons legend Jessie Tuggle at the end of 2000 forced Brooking to move to the middle linebacker position, and he filled those reasonably large shoes well.

From that point on, Brooking was one of the elite players in the NFL, ranking in the upper echelon every season. He was a Pro Bowl selection in five consecutive seasons (2001–2005), consistently proving himself as a leader for the Falcons defense.

In 2002 his 212 tackles made for an astounding moment in Atlanta history, forever sealing his name among franchise lore. He became a part of the fabled 200-tackle club, joining Jessie Tuggle, Tommy Nobis, Buddy Curry, and Fulton Kuykendall in the Falcons record books.

Even though he didn't receive a Pro Bowl selection during his last three years in Atlanta, he continued to put in impressive performances and recorded more than 100 tackles each season.

Brooking also made contributions off the field, founding the Keith Brooking Children's Foundation in 2003. With his mother acting as a foster parent while he was growing up, Brooking wanted to help give back to the foster children of metro Atlanta. He was even named as a nominee for the Home Depot NFL Neighborhood

MVP Award, which recognizes athletes who have extensive care and concern for their communities.

In 2007 Brooking was named to the Georgia Tech Athletic Hall of Fame, an honor that was a foregone conclusion. He parted ways with the Falcons in 2009 after 11 outstanding seasons, but his legacy continues to live on to this day. No matter where Brooking goes, he will always be remembered as a hometown hero.

William Andrews—a Sad, Injury-Shortened Career

William Andrews holds a special place in the history of the Atlanta Falcons. He is not only a part of the Falcons Ring of Honor, but he also was inducted to the Georgia Sports Hall of Fame after his playing days were over. Many claim him to be the greatest running back in the history of this franchise, and one can only speculate how much he could have achieved if his career hadn't been cut short by injury.

Andrews was born in Thomasville, Georgia, in 1955. He attended college at Auburn University and went on to be selected by Atlanta in Round 3 of the 1979 NFL Draft. It didn't take long for him to make an immediate impact with a franchise in need of some serious uplifting.

In 1979 he rushed for 1,023 yards on 239 carries, caught 39 passes for 309 yards, and finished with five touchdowns. He earned a spot on the NFL All-Rookie Team that year, but that was only the beginning of a five-year span that would blow every running back at the time out of the water.

One of the most memorable years of his career was 1980. Andrews finished with 1,308 yards, averaging 4.9 yards per carry.

Alongside quarterback Steve Bartkowski, he led the Falcons to their first division title in franchise history. The team went 12–4 that year, and even though they came up short against the Dallas Cowboys in the divisional round of the playoffs, it was the brightest moment in Falcons history at that point in time. Andrews made his first Pro Bowl that season as well, sparking another recurring trend. He would go on be a Pro Bowl selection the next three seasons in a row.

He finished with over 2,000 yards from scrimmage in 1981 and 1983, making him only the second player in NFL history to accomplish the feat of two 2,000-yard seasons. Atlanta made the playoffs again in the strike-shortened 1982 season. They only played nine games total, but Andrews continued to shine, boding well for the franchise's success going forward.

His most productive year out of the six NFL seasons he played came in 1983. After rushing for 1,567 yards, catching 59 balls for another 609 yards, and scoring 11 touchdowns, it looked like there was no stopping him. He was a monster in Atlanta's backfield and a nightmare for any team that lined up against him. The only thing that could stop him was the kryptonite of so many great athletes throughout history: his own body.

Andrews suffered a terrible knee injury in the 1984 preseason, and things were never the same from that point on. The injury was so severe that he was unable to play for two consecutive seasons. He didn't see one snap in 1984 or 1985. He didn't quit, though; there was no way he was just going to throw in the towel. By 1986 he was finally able to see action again. Unfortunately, that knee would never be the same, nor would Andrews.

In 15 games played in 1986, Andrews did not start once. He was only given 52 carries, which he turned into 214 yards and a lone score. By the end of the 1986 season he understood that things were never going to be the same. William Andrews hung up his cleats and never stepped on to the field again. He retired in 1987, ending a career that had so much potential.

Today he sits in second place in the Falcons record book for rushing yards (5,986) and is tied for sixth in career touchdowns (41). The Georgia Sports Hall of Fame called his name in 1996, and the Falcons inducted him into their Ring of Honor in 2004.

If you ask any Falcons fan who the best running back in the history of the franchise is, Andrews' name is likely to be mentioned the majority of the time. He could lay the hit on defenders and run straight through them. He had the vision and tenacity to set himself apart from the rest of the field. Those who don't know the name or never had the privilege of watching him play are truly missing out on a great period of history here in Atlanta. Speculation constantly revolves around this man and how great he could have been. It's tough to imagine how much he could have accomplished if he had stayed healthy, if that knee had been able to recover. Four All-Pro seasons in a row is nothing short of spectacular, and things were only looking up from there.

The Falcons have experienced some truly adverse times through-out the course of their history, but William Andrews brought a new sense of hope to the entire city. After leading Atlanta to its first division title in history and setting records that still keep his name in the books today, he is an integral part of this franchise's history and a name with which every fan should be familiar.

22 The 200-Tackle Club

Statistics are sometimes noted at the discretion of each individual franchise. Different sources will always have different numbers and figures for varying players. As far as tackles go, each individual team will keep records on the amount their players finish with. The Atlanta Falcons official website has a full archive of anything and everything one could possibly wonder about the franchise's history, and sure enough statistics on individual tackles are in there as well.

In the sport of football there are plenty of records that are no easy feat to obtain, but as far as tackles go, reaching the 200 mark is one of the most prestigious accomplishments an athlete can achieve. As the Falcons have a rich history of talented linebackers, they also have a fair share of stars who have accomplished the task of hitting the 200 benchmark in the tackles category. Tommy Nobis, Fulton Kuykendall, Buddy Curry, Jessie Tuggle, and Keith Brooking have all seen their names go down in the record books as members of the Falcons 200-tackle club, making for a rather prominent group of guys.

Even though only five players have reached 200 or more tackles in the history of the Falcons, the very first man to do it reached the mark in the very first year of the franchise. Tommy Nobis was drafted by Atlanta with the No. 1 overall pick in 1966. He was an incredible defender for the Texas Longhorns in college, and with his track record, it was no surprise he was the first pick. In 1965 he won the Maxwell Award, Outland Trophy, and finished seventh in the voting for the Heisman Trophy. The Falcons were not going to pass up an athlete of his stature.

Nobis' rookie season in the NFL was 1966, and it was hard to believe the impact he made right away. He finished the year with 296 total tackles. For his efforts he was named the NFL Defensive Rookie of the Year and received a Pro Bowl roster spot, an honor he would see come his way four more times in his career.

As it stands today, 296 tackles sits at the top of the record books in Atlanta. Nobis set the bar pretty high by putting up those numbers in his/Atlanta's first season.

The next man to reach 200 tackles didn't break Nobis' record, but he certainly came close. Fulton Kuykendall wasn't a highly coveted prospect coming out of college like Nobis, but he made the most of his playing time when he made it to the next level. Kuykendall made up for his lack of elite athleticism with his tenacity and determination on the field. He didn't care what he had to do, he was tackling the man with the ball.

During his fourth season with the Falcons, he made a serious run at the all-time record for tackles. In 1978 Atlanta reached the playoffs for the first time ever, and Kuykendall was part of the driving force on defense. He finished with 284 tackles that season, just 12 shy of Nobis' total. Kuykendall didn't receive any major accolades during his Falcons tenure, but he is certainly regarded as a great player in the history of the team.

Just a few seasons after Kuykendall hit 284, Buddy Curry stepped up into the spotlight. Curry made his way to Atlanta in the second round of the 1980 NFL Draft and quickly made a name for himself as the top tackler year after year.

Curry was the NFL Defensive Rookie of the Year after he completed his first season, and he was an All-Pro selection in 1980 and 1982. Surprisingly, though, he didn't receive any of the honors in the season when he had his best statistical performance. In 1983 Curry really took off, finishing with 229 total tackles overall. Curry led the Falcons in tackles in six seasons with the team, but his 229 tackles boosted him into the 200-tackle club, making him the third member.

After Curry hit the mark in the early 1980s, Atlanta waited seven years to see their next player hit the heralded 200. Jessie Tuggle is one of the most widely recognized names through the decades of Falcons greats, and he gained entry to the 200-tackle club in 1990. He finished with 201 tackles in his fourth year with the team, but he didn't stop there.

Tuggle became the first Falcon to ever record 200 or more tackles in multiple years. He followed up his 1990 performance with 207 tackles in 1991. It seemed as though one year wasn't enough. Tuggle was going to start his own club for two-time 200-tacklers.

He went on to make the Pro Bowl five times and ultimately was inducted into the Falcons Ring of Honor. Tuggle proved that if to really make a lasting impression, a player should reach 200 tackles more than once.

The last and final player, at least to this day, to reach 200 tackles is another hometown superstar. Like Tuggle, he basically spent his entire life in the state of Georgia. Keith Brooking played his college ball at Georgia Tech, and he racked up the stats during his four seasons as a Yellow Jacket.

He became the team's leading tackler for eight seasons in a row between 2001 and 2008, but two years in particular stood out. Brooking finished with 212 tackles in 2002 and 207 tackles the following season. He followed up Tuggle's act with a similar performance, and he made the Pro Bowl five times as well.

The last time the Falcons saw a player achieve 200 or more tackles was in 2003. No one has been close since that historic year for Brooking, but there will surely be more to come in the future, as Atlanta has a tendency to draft linebackers who make the most of their playing time.

Falcons' First Win: November 20, 1966

The city of Atlanta experienced an era of change in the 1960s. It was a time of expansion for the heart of Georgia, and Atlanta was rapidly becoming one of the premier cities in the country on many different levels. The Braves moved their franchise from Milwaukee down to the South in 1966, a change that had been in the works for some time up until that point. A baseball team, though, wasn't the only new addition brewing at the time. Rankin M. Smith was pushing hard for a football franchise to start up, and he finally saw his dream come true with the Atlanta Falcons, whose inaugural season was 1966. At the cost of $8.5 million, the NFL awarded Smith with the franchise, making Atlanta the 23rd professional football team in existence at the time.

As with any startup franchise, it's never easy to experience success right away. Things take time to fall into place. No expansion team ever comes out of the gates and blows everyone away from the first day. This certainly was the case for the Falcons, as their first win did not arrive until 10 games into the first year.

Expansion teams are awarded several luxuries, such as having the first pick in the NFL Draft. The Falcons chose to go with Tommy Nobis, a young linebacker out of the University of Texas. In time, the city would come to see that this selection was one of the best in the history of the franchise.

Smith and his club also possessed the No. 16 overall pick coming at the end of the first round, and with it they drafted quarterback Randy Johnson. Johnson would ultimately become the man to help lead the Falcons to their first win in the history of... well...ever.

The first game ever played by Atlanta actually turned out to be a hard-fought battle in which the Falcons nearly pulled out a win. A matchup against the Los Angeles Rams drew an opening-day crowd of 54,418 fans at Atlanta Stadium (which would eventually be named Atlanta–Fulton County Stadium).

The Rams jumped out to at 16–0 lead, but the Falcons managed to claw their way back into the contest, scoring 14 unanswered points to pull them within two. A late field goal, though, put the game on ice for L.A. and sent Atlanta packing with the first loss for the franchise. A victory would have been quite a remarkable

The Flightless Falcons

The Falcons had a training camp for this bird. It was coached up.
It knew pass patterns...or perhaps the fly pattern. It was going to
be quite a sideshow for the first game of the NFL team in 1966 at
Atlanta–Fulton County Stadium.

This falcon—one with wings, not legs and shoulder pads—was
going to fly around the stadium three times and make a dramatic landing.
The crowd was going to roar, and the team was going to take off.

Whoops.

The Falcon was hijacked by free will. It never came back and
soared away instead.

On September 11, 1966, the Falcons lost to the Los Angeles
Rams, 19–14.

beginning to the latest addition to the NFL, but it just wasn't
meant to be.

Speaking of meant to be, it appeared as if the entire season
wasn't meant to be early on. The Falcons were young and inex-
perienced, but they just couldn't seem to pull it together to spark
that first taste of success. Following the initial nail-biter, the Birds
dropped the next eight games in a row, losing each by double digits.

No one anticipated a Super Bowl season, but things got pretty
rough at times. On October 16 San Francisco demolished the
Falcons 44–7 at home. The very next weekend Atlanta was routed
in Green Bay, leaving the field with the scoreboard reading 56–3.
It was hardly something a start-up team wanted to see, along with
a fresh young fan base waiting in the wings.

At 0–9 there remained just five games left of the schedule, just
five matchups to find that first triumph. The day of achievement
finally reared its head on November 20, as the Falcons took on the
New York Football Giants at Yankee Stadium.

Johnson and his boys took the lead early, as the rookie quarterback fired a nine-yard strike to running back Ernie Wheelwright
to open up a 7–0 lead. Johnson connected again for another

touchdown, this time to Vern Burke in the second quarter. Atlanta headed to the locker room at halftime leading 13–3. The question on everyone's mind lingered: *Can this finally be it?*

As it turned out, they made it happen. Head coach Norb Hecker rallied his troops and kept the ball moving in the second half. The Falcons took a 20–3 lead in the third quarter after yet another touchdown pass from Johnson. The Giants attempted to make a game of it, but Atlanta wasn't going to let this one slip away. As the final seconds ran off, the Falcons knew they had finally made it to the promised land, winning 27–16. Not only was it the first victory in the team's history, but they managed to pull it off by double digits.

Hecker and the boys fared well in the last five games of the year, finishing with a 3–2 record during that period. Even more surprising, the Falcons did not finish in last place, putting them in the record books as the only expansion team at that time to not finish at the very bottom.

Tommy Nobis won Rookie of the Year and was named to the Pro Bowl, and the city of Atlanta averaged 56,526 people in attendance for the Falcons home games. They didn't make the playoffs, they didn't win the Super Bowl, and they surely didn't come anywhere near a winning record. One thing was certain, though: the city of Atlanta had a promising young team that was heading in the right direction as 1966 came to a close.

24 Finally, Back-to-Back Winning Seasons

One of the least-talked-about feats across the NFL—and for good reason—was the fact that it was 2009, and the Atlanta

Falcons hadn't posted back-to-back winning seasons in franchise history.

The Falcons were entering their 44th season and hadn't had consecutive seasons with a winning record. Folks in Atlanta knew, but it's not like that kind of statistic was something anyone outside of the city—or the region, for that matter—could really believe. How could a franchise go that long without having back-to-back winning seasons?

Up to that point, the closest Atlanta had been to posting back-to-back winning seasons was in 2005. After an 11–5 campaign in 2004 put the Falcons in the playoffs and ultimately the NFC Championship Game, the Falcons were on the verge of getting back to the postseason. In the season's first 13 games, the Falcons stood at 8–5 and essentially in control of their own destiny.

But in Week 15, Atlanta lost 16–3 to Chicago, a game that saw Falcons quarterback Michael Vick finish 13-for-32, passing for 122 yards and two interceptions. The following week, the Falcons lost 27–24 to Tampa Bay in overtime. And in Week 17 Carolina blew out Atlanta 44–11, effectively ending what once seemed like a surefire bid to capture two consecutive winning seasons. Adding insult to injury, Tampa Bay and Carolina both finished 11–5 and made appearances in the playoffs.

But that was then, and 2009 was the year for Atlanta to erase the painful memories of the past, which included more losing seasons than winning. Atlanta opened the season 2–0, defeating Miami and Carolina in the first two weeks. A trip to New England, however, gave the Falcons their first loss. The Patriots pulled a rabbit out of the Bill Belichick hat of magic tricks, electing to utilize three-tight-end sets all game—something Atlanta wasn't prepared for.

Throughout the season, it was a bit of a tug-of-war for Atlanta. Some weeks it looked great, other weeks it appeared the team needed a little more seasoning before making the deep run many pundits had predicted heading into 2009. Atlanta was 4–1 but then dropped consecutive games to Dallas and New Orleans, the latter in a heartbreaking 35–27 loss at the Superdome. The Falcons were able to get back on the winning track, getting to 5–3 for the season after defeating Washington 31–17 in Week 9.

But just like they had done earlier in the season, the Falcons traded wins for losses, dropping their next two against Carolina and the New York Giants. The loss against Carolina saw running back Michael Turner suffer a high ankle sprain, limiting his playing time and effectiveness for the remainder of the season. The Giants loss, though, hurt particularly badly. On the road at the Meadowlands, Atlanta was playing from behind the entire way. Early in the fourth quarter, the Falcons faced a 31–17 deficit but continued to fight. Receiver Eric Weems caught a four-yard pass from quarterback Matt Ryan with 6:01 remaining to cut the Giants' lead to 31–24. The Falcons gave up one first down on New York's ensuing possession before forcing a punt, giving Atlanta a chance to tie the game with 3:42 remaining.

Beginning at Atlanta's own 24, Ryan went to work, completing five of his first seven passes to move the Falcons to the Giants 24-yard line with 1:23 remaining. After an incomplete pass on first down, Ryan found veteran receiver Marty Booker for a seven-yard gain. On third-and-three, Ryan hit tight end Tony Gonzalez for a six-yard gain to get Atlanta to New York's 11-yard line. Following the play, Atlanta called a timeout to stop the clock with 39 seconds remaining.

It should've been clear to the Giants who Ryan would look for coming out of the timeout. Of Ryan's 10 previous passes, three were completed to Gonzalez for 26 yards. On first down, Ryan went Gonzalez's way but was unable to connect. On second down, Ryan found him in the middle of the field for the tying touchdown with a little more than 30 seconds to go, ultimately sending the game to overtime. Atlanta was riding the momentum and looked

Falcons Records after a Winning Season

As you can from the table below, the Atlanta Falcons produced 10 winning seasons between 1971 and 2005 without being able to follow up with a winning season the next year.

The closest season was in 1972, when the Falcons lost their last two games to go 7–7 after a 7–6–1 season in 1971.

In 2005 the team lost to Carolina in its final game of the season to finish 8–8 after an 11–5 2004 season.

1971: 7–6–1	1982: 5–4	2002: 9–6–1
1972: 7–7	1983: 7–9	2003: 5–11
1973: 9–5	1991: 10–6	2004: 11–5
1974: 3–11	1992: 6–10	2005: 8–8
1978: 9–7	1995: 9–7	2008: 11–5
1979: 6–10	1996: 3–13	2009: 9–7
1980: 12–4	1998: 14–2	2010: 13–3
1981: 7–9	1999: 5–11	

to have finally gained control of a game controlled by the Giants until that point.

However, it wasn't meant to be for Atlanta. New York won the overtime coin toss and elected to receive. The Giants began their first drive with decent field position, thanks to a 34-yard return to the Giants 33-yard line by receiver Domenik Hixon. The Giants picked up a first down before quarterback Eli Manning found receiver Mario Manningham for a 29-yard gain to get down to Atlanta's 23. Four plays later, kicker Lawrence Tynes kicked a 36-yarder through the uprights to give the Giants a 34–31 win.

A week later, Atlanta rebounded to the tune of a 20–17 win over Tampa Bay, despite the fact that Ryan suffered a turf-toe injury on the third play from scrimmage that required backup Chris Redman to finish in his place. In dramatic fashion, the game came down to the final seconds again, but with Atlanta pulling out a win this time. Redman found receiver Roddy White for a five-yard touchdown pass with 23 seconds to go to escape the Buccaneers' grasp.

But without Ryan a week later against Philadelphia, Atlanta struggled as the Eagles ran away with a 34–7 victory. Vick, Atlanta's former franchise quarterback who was released from his contract stemming from his involvement in a dogfighting ring, threw for one touchdown and ran for another in Philadelphia's win. Redman and White saved the game from ending in a shutout with a meaningless touchdown as the clock struck triple zeros, in what could be considered Atlanta's lowest point of 2009.

Sitting at 6–6, the Falcons needed a win against New Orleans to keep its playoff hopes alive. Atlanta did all it could, with Redman, still filling in for Ryan, throwing for 303 yards. The Falcons even had two drives in the fourth quarter to either tie the Saints with a field goal or move ahead with a touchdown. Atlanta did neither and lost 26–23. The Saints remained undefeated until the following week, when they lost to Dallas—which ironically knocked the Falcons out of playoff contention. At that point the Falcons were playing for pride and for a shot at a second consecutive winning season.

A day after the Saints' loss to the Cowboys, the Falcons were set to play the Jets on the road in snowy New Jersey. The outside conditions were so bad, even by Northeastern standards, that the two teams played to a somewhat empty stadium.

The weather also played a major role into the defensive struggle that saw Jets quarterback Mark Sanchez toss three interceptions and Ryan, back from his turf-toe injury, finish the game with a 69.7 quarterback rating. With the Jets leading 7–3 late in the fourth quarter, the Falcons went to work. On a third-and-nine from Atlanta's 42, Ryan found White for 16 yards. Jets defensive back Donald Strickland aided Atlanta's cause by grabbing White's face mask, giving the Falcons 15 free yards. At the

Jets 27, backup running back Jason Snelling ran for a 20-yard gain to get down to the 7. But in Atlanta's next three plays, the team could only muster one yard. The Falcons faced a fourth-and-six, with a winning season on the line. Atlanta called timeout to mull things over.

Just as against the Giants, the Jets should've had a good idea who Ryan would try to find in a short-yardage situation with the game winding down. Gonzalez, lined up on the right side of the line of scrimmage, ran straight to the goal line before breaking right into his out route. Perfectly timed and open, Ryan hit Gonzalez just over the goal line for the go-ahead score. Up 10–7, Brent Grimes intercepted Sanchez on the Jets' last-ditch effort. Atlanta was able to leave the Meadowlands with a win.

Finding its stride for the first time all season, Atlanta's defense stifled Buffalo a week later in a 31–3 win. The Falcons were 8–7 and just one win away from their second consecutive winning season.

In Week 17, the Falcons faced a Tampa Bay team looking to get even with Atlanta, who had escaped the two teams' previous meeting with a 20–17 win. After trading field goals in the first two quarters, Atlanta went up 10–3 after Ryan found tight end Justin Peelle for a two-yard touchdown with no time remaining in the first half. Both teams were scoreless in the third quarter, highlighted by Tampa Bay blocking a 40-yard attempt from Falcons kicker Matt Bryant. The Falcons defense was stout, holding the Buccaneers to just one first down in the third quarter.

But Tampa Bay evened the score in the fourth quarter, as Bucs quarterback Josh Freeman found receiver Antonio Bryant for an eight-yard touchdown reception to even the score at 10–10.

Atlanta did itself no favors on its next possession, as Ryan threw an interception on a third-and-two to Bucs safety Sabby Piscitelli. But Falcons cornerback Chris Owens bailed out his team by picking off Freeman on the next play, which he returned 13 yards to Tampa Bay's 43-yard line. Just five plays later, Ryan found White in the end zone for a 12-yard touchdown.

Freeman then drove the Bucs down to Atlanta's 35-yard line before launching a pass to the end zone, intended for Antonio Bryant again. But Grimes was there for the interception and touchback. Atlanta then ran nine plays and saw Bryant nail a 36-yard field goal to put the Falcons up 20–10, icing the game away with a minute left to play.

It wasn't a pretty season, and it was considered disappointing without a playoff appearance. But it was a huge weight lifted off Atlanta's shoulders. No longer would the locals have to wonder when the Falcons would finally capture back-to-back winning seasons. And no longer would this statistic be a surprising talking point to those around the country.

"We want to be a relevant football team year in and year out, and that's what we talk about," coach Mike Smith said following the Week 17 win over Tampa Bay. "When you're relevant, you've got to have a winning record, and then you'll have an opportunity to be in the discussion for the playoffs. We weren't in the playoffs this year, but we have a season that gave us nine wins. That's something that we're very proud of."

In the two seasons that followed, Atlanta posted winning seasons of 13–3 in 2010 and 10–6 in 2011. Each featured a trip to the playoffs. What was once a monumental feat is now expected.

Norb Hecker: Atlanta's First Head Coach

When the Falcons were founded and purchased in 1965, local sportswriters began speculating who Rankin M. Smith would hire as the team's first head football coach. Plenty of names were thrown out for consideration, including University of Arkansas coach Frank Broyles, former San Francisco 49ers coach Red Hickey, Green Bay Packers coach Vince Lombardi, and former Cleveland Browns coach Paul Brown, among others.

So when the Falcons made their decision, it was quite the surprise to most folks around the league. Atlanta tried but was unable to land Lombardi, and the story goes that Lombardi didn't recommend anyone on his staff for a head coaching gig when Smith asked. Smith decided to offer the job to Lombardi's assistant, Norb Hecker, anyway, seeing that if he was an understudy to Lombardi, he must be a solid hire.

Hecker was 39 at the time he was hired after spending seven years with Lombardi. With Green Bay, Hecker was a part of three world championship teams and four conference winners. With Atlanta, it was a much different story.

In Atlanta's first exhibition game against the Philadelphia Eagles, kicker Wade Traynham set the tone for Hecker's tenure. On the opening kickoff—or lack thereof—Traynham swung his leg and missed the ball completely. The Falcons dropped that first preseason game to Philadelphia 9–7. In the regular season, Hecker's Falcons squad lost their first nine games before stumbling into the win column in Week 10 against the Giants. Atlanta ended its inaugural season at a futile 3–11.

Hecker's squad wasn't expected to compete with the rest of the league immediately. But in his second season, Smith was at least hoping to see signs of improvement from his head coach. After Atlanta's first six games, the Falcons were 0–5–1 and looking worse than they had a year earlier. In Week 7 Atlanta got its lone win that season by defeating the Minnesota Vikings 21–20. But the winning ways ended there, as the Falcons lost the remainder of their games and ended the 1967 season 1–12–1.

It was do or die for Hecker in 1968. He needed to win, and he needed to win fast. But in Week 1, the Falcons were blown out by the Vikings 47–7 as Hecker's future looked more and more bleak each day. The Baltimore Colts and San Francisco 49ers then posted wins over Atlanta in the next two weeks, leaving Hecker with an 0–3 record to begin the 1968 season. That was enough for Smith, who fired Hecker in the midst of a 10-game losing streak that stretched over two seasons. On October 1, 1968, the Falcons hired former Vikings coach Norm Van Brocklin to replace Hecker. He went on to finish 4–26–1 in two seasons plus three games.

Before becoming an assistant coach with Green Bay, Hecker possessed an NFL pedigree, having played as a safety for the Los Angeles Rams and the Washington Redskins after playing college football at Baldwin-Wallace College. After Atlanta fired him, Hecker became a defensive backs coach with the Giants. Hecker later was an assistant coach who transitioned into a front-office position with the San Francisco 49ers teams that won four Super Bowls in the 1980s. He ended his coaching career as an assistant for the Amsterdam Admirals of the World League of American Football in the mid-1990s.

Hecker lost his battle with cancer and passed away at the age of 76 on March 14, 2004. Hecker may not have had the success he dreamed of when he became the Falcons' first football coach, but he still leaves the legacy of being the first coach of a professional football team in the city of Atlanta.

Mike Kenn: No One's Played More Games for the Falcons

Selected with the 13th overall pick in the 1978 draft, the Falcons got their money's worth with offensive tackle Mike Kenn, an iron man of sorts who rarely missed playing time and always came through when needed. Every game Kenn played in, he started.

Kenn's toughness as a football player began as a walk-on at the University of Michigan, where he played for legendary coach Bo Schembechler. At Michigan, Kenn went from walking on to the storied program to earning All–Big Ten honors twice in the 1976 and 1977 seasons. A native of Evanston, Illinois, Kenn was forced to move away from the Midwest when the Falcons selected him.

Kenn, a 6'7", 275-pound offensive tackle, broke into the starting lineup immediately as a rookie. He started each game in his rookie season and helped an offensive line produce 1,660 rushing yards for the year. Call Kenn the good-luck charm Atlanta needed, as the Falcons made their first playoff appearance in 1978. The Falcons defeated the Philadelphia Eagles 14–13 in the wild-card round before losing 27–20 to the Dallas Cowboys in the divisional round.

Kenn hit his stride by 1980, becoming a mean and nasty figure on the Atlanta offensive line. From 1980 to 1984, Kenn reached the Pro Bowl each year. Kenn blocked for some talented running backs who had big seasons for Atlanta. In 1983 William Andrews ran for 1,567 yards and seven touchdowns, earning Pro Bowl honors along with Kenn. From 1984 to 1986 Kenn opened holes for running back Gerald Riggs, who ran for more than 1,000 yards each of those seasons, including 1,719 yards in 1985, which was a franchise record until Michael Turner ran for 1,799 yards in 2008.

Mike Kenn (79) prepares to battle AFC defensive end Art Still of the Kansas City Chiefs during the 1982 NFL Pro Bowl played on January 31, 1982, at Aloha Stadium in Honolulu, Hawaii.

Kenn played 17 seasons for Atlanta, the second-most of any player in franchise history. His 251 career games, all of which he's started, ranks as the most any Falcons player has ever played and started in. The 251 starts puts Kenn tied for seventh place in NFL history with former NFL offensive tackle Lomas Brown. Kenn's final season was in 1994, which capped his entire career in Atlanta. In 2008 the Falcons inducted Kenn and his No. 78 into the Falcons' famed Ring of Honor. Kenn, along with former Falcons quarterback Steve Bartkowski, is also a member of the National Polish-American Hall of Fame.

Kenn has been a three-time nominee for the Pro Football Hall of Fame, which didn't contain any Falcons players until cornerback Deion Sanders, who spent the first five seasons of his 14-year career in Atlanta, was inducted with the 2011 class. He was the NFL's Man of the Year in 1990 and served as the president of the NFL Player's Association from 1989 to 1996.

After retiring from football, Kenn remained in the Atlanta area. He entered politics and won an election to become the chairman of the Fulton County Commission in 1998. In 2003 Kenn resigned from this position to become the president of the nonprofit organization Georgians for Better Transportation.

The Catch That Gave Atlanta Its First Winning Season

Heading into the final week of the 1971 season, the Atlanta Falcons sat at 6–6–1.

The six wins tied a franchise record for wins in a season, but after a 21-point loss to the San Francisco 49ers the week prior, the Falcons' outside shot at sneaking into the playoffs evaporated. Atlanta's best chance at setting the bar just a little higher was beating the New Orleans Saints on the final weekend of the season to give the Falcons their first winning season in franchise history.

The Falcons had already played the Saints earlier in the year and won 28–6. The Saints were 4–7–2 heading into the game, so hopes were high for the Falcons.

Coach Norm Van Brocklin told the *Rome News-Tribune* that a win against New Orleans would be a "sign of progress" for the

Ken Burrow Shined with a Broken Wrist

It wasn't enough that rookie wide receiver Ken Burrow, with 34 seconds left to play in the game, caught the touchdown pass that gave the Atlanta Falcons their first-ever winning season; Burrow was also playing with a broken wrist.

Burrow broke his wrist in a Week 2 game against the Los Angeles Rams and played the final 11 games of the season with that injury.

Not only did Burrow make that historic catch, he twice posted 190 yards receiving in a game and caught 30 passes, all after the injury.

six-year-old franchise but warned that the Saints were "the most improved team in the division" and were "considerably better than they were when we played them earlier."

Van Brocklin set the table on the day prior to the game, and tensions were high.

The teams played to a 10-all tie at halftime and Saints quarterback Archie Manning rushed for a six-yard score to give New Orleans a 17–10 lead going into the fourth quarter.

The Saints had dominated the game to that point, even if the score showed it was close. New Orleans gained more yardage on the ground and through the air and looked poised to ruin Atlanta's chances at a winning season.

Atlanta quarterback Bob Berry took matters into his own hands in the fourth quarter. With less than six minutes to play in the game, Berry hit Ken Burrow on an 84-yard pass that positioned the Falcons on the Saints 3-yard line. Art Malone drove the ball into the end zone from one yard out, tying the game at 17.

But Atlanta's special teams hiccupped, allowing Saints rookie return man Virgil Robinson to return the ensuing kickoff to midfield. With just more than three minutes to play, Saints kicker Charlie Durkee gave the lead back to New Orleans with a 36-yard field goal.

Answering in turn, Falcons return specialist Jim "Cannonball" Butler took the Saints' kickoff and carried it back to the Atlanta 49-yard line. Atlanta had just more than three minutes to score.

Prior to the scoring pass, the most vital play of the final drive came on third-and-18 from the New Orleans 45. Berry hit wide receiver Wes Chesson on a 19-yard pass pattern that was measured perfectly for the situation.

With 34 seconds left to play, from the Saints 22-yard line, Berry connected with the rookie Burrow in the end zone to give Atlanta the win and secure its first winning season in franchise history. It was Berry's only touchdown throw of the game.

For Burrow, the catch not only secured a winning season for his team, but the moment was statistically significant as well. Those final 22 yards gave Burrow 190 for the day, a season high that Burrow never eclipsed in his five-year career. His eight catches in the game also lasted as a career high for the young receiver.

28 1983: The Year of the Comeback

The Atlanta Falcons went 7–9 during the 1983 NFL season and finished in last place in the NFC West division. Even though Falcons fans endured a last-place finish, it could have been a lot worse had Atlanta not found a way to come from behind four times to win football games that year.

The 1983 season should be remembered for some personal accolades. Quarterback Steve Bartkowski threw for 3,167 yards and 22 touchdowns, the third-highest total in both categories for his career.

Running back William Andrews rushed for 1,567 yards, the highest single-season total of his career. Andrews also caught 59 passes and was voted onto the NFC Pro Bowl team.

The Falcons had another Pro Bowler in Billy "White Shoes" Johnson that season. It was Johnson's only Pro Bowl season with the Falcons, and he led the team with 64 receptions that year. Johnson also returned a punt for a touchdown.

Even though all three of those players shined personally, it was the group effort of the team—and the offense in particular—that stood out.

The Falcons won just seven times in 1983, but four times the team had to come from behind. In each of those four come-from-behind wins. Atlanta was trailing as it entered the fourth quarter.

In Week 1 the Falcons erased a 17–13 fourth-quarter Chicago Bears lead to win 20–17. In Week 8 Atlanta trailed the New York Jets 21–7 heading into the fourth quarter and scored 20 points in the last quarter to win 27–21.

Four weeks later the Falcons trailed San Francisco 17–14 heading into the fourth quarter and pulled out a 28–24 win. And the very next week Atlanta was behind 31–24 to Green Bay after three quarters and won the game 47–41 in overtime.

As crazy as having four come-from-behind wins in the same season with just seven wins total is, two of those stand out even more.

In the Week 8 win over the Jets and the Week 13 win over the Packers, both times Atlanta allowed its opponent to jump out to a 21–0 lead. Erasing a 21-point lead ranks at the top of the Falcons history book in regard to largest comeback wins ever, and both instances are tied for first place.

In Atlanta's win over the Jets, Bartkowski threw two touchdown passes in less than three minutes, and then Johnson tied the game on a 71-yard punt return for a touchdown. Mick Luckhurst iced the game for Atlanta with a 32-yard field goal with just less than four minutes to play.

For Atlanta's second 21-point comeback of the 1983 season, Kenny Johnson returned two interceptions for touchdowns. The first interception, a 26-yard touchdown return, came in the fourth quarter and put the Falcons ahead of Green Bay 41–34. Johnson's second came just more than two minutes into the overtime period. He picked off a pass and ran it back 31 yards for the game-winning score.

The 1983 Falcons sure did know excitement.

Two-Sport Stars: Sanders and Jordan

The 1990s were the golden years for the multitasker. Personal computers were coming into their own, and the Internet was becoming popular. It's no surprise that the two-sport star rose to fame during this decade.

Although the name Bo Jackson still brings back fond memories for thousands of fans, *two* Atlanta Falcons managed to pull off successful careers in both baseball and football.

One was a speedy slap hitter in baseball and a Hall of Famer as a cornerback. The other was a hard-hitting safety for three years before moving on to a terrific career in Major League Baseball. I'm writing, of course, about Brian Jordan and Deion Sanders—two of the greatest two-sport stars who ever lived. These are their stories:

Brian Jordan

It's rare that a player winds up playing in baseball's minor leagues and for a pro football team at the same time. Brian Jordan can say he's done it.

The Buffalo Bills drafted the hard-nosed Richmond Spiders safety in the seventh round in 1988, while the St. Louis Cardinals chose him in the first round of the amateur draft. While he worked his way up through the Cardinals minor league system, Jordan was cut by the Bills and moved on to the Falcons.

He had a huge impact in Atlanta, starting 30 games at safety in two seasons and providing a hard-hitting presence in the defensive backfield. He also intercepted five passes and caused two safeties, endearing himself to fans and coaches alike.

But Jordan's heart was with baseball. After three seasons with the Falcons, he walked away from the team and away from the big hits he delivered every Sunday to sign a major league contract with the MLB's St. Louis Cardinals. He wound up playing 15 seasons in the bigs, finishing his career with a stellar .282/.333/.455 slash line, 184 home runs, 821 runs batted in, and 119 stolen bases.

Jordan never became a Hall of Famer in either sport, but he's one of the few players to play both sports at a high level. Falcons fans can only wonder what might have been if Jordan had chosen to play football his whole career.

Deion Sanders

It is Sanders who had the Hall of Fame football career. He also managed a nine-year career in the major leagues—an astonishing accomplishment. Along the way, he established himself as a flamboyant performer on and off the field and one of the few shutdown cornerbacks in the NFL. He was the toast of the town, and with good reason.

A two-sport star at Florida State, Sanders' career start was the opposite of Jordan's. He was drafted in the 30th round of the MLB amateur draft in 1989 by the New York Yankees, who saw a raw baseball player with tantalizing speed. But the Atlanta Falcons saw huge potential for the young Sanders at cornerback and drafted him accordingly, making him the fifth player selected overall in 1989.

While he didn't pay dividends in MLB until his breakout year in 1992 with the Atlanta Braves, Sanders was a star with the Falcons from the first moment his cleats hit the turf. He tallied five interceptions and a kick return for a touchdown in 1989, quickly cementing a legacy as "Neon" Deion, the man who electrified a city.

Fans were equally enthralled during his next four seasons, which saw Sanders pick 19 more passes over that span. He was the best player on the field for the team during its amazing 1991 season, when the Falcons advanced to the playoffs before losing to the eventual Super Bowl–champion Washington Redskins.

During the height of his career with the Falcons, Sanders was a true multisport hero for Atlanta, ringing up a .304 batting average with the Braves in 1992. As speedy on the base paths as he was when shadowing wide receivers, he hit a career-high eight home runs that year.

Unfortunately for the Atlanta fans who adored him, Sanders passed his last full season in a Falcons and Braves jersey just a year later. He went on to have a career as a shutdown corner with the San Francisco 49ers, the Dallas Cowboys, and the Washington Redskins and plied his hitting skills with the Cincinnati Reds and San Francisco Giants.

His baseball career ended in 2001, while his football career took him through 2005. His combined 23 years between the NFL and MLB is a testament to his talent and incredible drive.

In 2011 Sanders was inducted into the Pro Football Hall of Fame and the Atlanta Falcons' Ring of Honor. Now an announcer and pitchman par excellence, he remains a true Falcons legend.

For these dual-sport stars, Atlanta was a wonderful place to start a football career.

30 Rolland Lawrence: A Cover Corner Like No Other

Sometimes greatness comes and goes too quickly. Such is the case of Rolland Lawrence, one of the greatest cornerbacks the Atlanta Falcons ever had.

Lawrence's playing career only spanned eight seasons, but he made the most of them. One of the premier—and most underappreciated—cornerbacks of his era, Lawrence made only one Pro Bowl, in 1977.

It's fair to argue that the man known to friends and fans as "Bay" deserved many more. Possessing no spectacular size or speed, Lawrence became a force of nature in the secondary through sheer will and impossibly hard work.

Making the team out of tiny Tabor College as an undrafted free agent was no easy task, just one of the many challenges the 5'10" Lawrence overcame in his career. Before his retirement in 1980, he also conquered countless NFL wide receivers and history itself.

In the beginning, Lawrence was just an intriguing prospect. He played in all 14 games in his 1973 rookie season but did not crack the starting lineup behind the immortal Ken Reaves and his confident counterpart Tom Hayes, who picked four passes. Still, his talent shone through, and when the Falcons traded away Reaves in 1974 following a labor spat, Lawrence got his job.

He silently flashed excellent coverage skills that year but only picked one more pass. Those two mostly quiet years made 1975 even more surprising. That year, Lawrence exploded onto the national scene, intercepting a career-high nine passes and being named as an All-Pro for the first time. His aggressive style and evident athleticism made him the scourge of receivers across the NFL for the first time, but it was not the last.

Lawrence went on to intercept at least six passes per season for the next four years, piling up a total of 25 over that span. In 1977 the Falcons put together one of the greatest defenses in NFL history, the legendary Gritz Blitz.

Lawrence led the way by shutting down opposing receivers and picking seven passes in the most surprising defensive turnaround in the league's history. The year before, the Falcons had been putrid on defense, allowing 312 points in 14 games and getting whipped 59–0 by the Los Angeles Rams. In 1977 they allowed only 129 points in 14 games, a new NFL record and one that would stand forever. Somehow, this wonderful, improbable team led by Leeman Bennett missed the playoffs, but Lawrence and his teammates had a season to remember.

But Lawrence wasn't done. In 1978 and 1979, he again punished opposing quarterbacks foolish enough to throw to his side of the field, racking up six interceptions in each season. By then, his reputation had been cemented, and teams began to avoid him. There is no greater sign of respect for a cornerback, and it was richly deserved. He also showed off ever-growing confidence as a tackler.

Lawrence played one more season, wrapping up his Falcons career with three interceptions in a full 16 games, before walking away from the game forever at the age of 29. In just eight seasons, he pulled down a franchise-record 39 interceptions and still holds the team's secondary record for forced fumbles with 13. He was a onetime Pro Bowler and onetime All-Pro, and in a more just world, he would have been recognized more frequently. He could still be entered into the team's Ring of Honor in the future, as he spent all eight of his seasons with the Falcons.

Fans and his peers are left to wonder how Lawrence would have fared had he kept playing into his thirties. One thing seems certain: Lawrence's records are likely to never be broken. That, in and of itself, is a testament to his remarkable career.

From undrafted free agent to prolific cornerback, Rolland Lawrence rose to heights few cornerbacks will ever be able to boast. He, too, is a true Atlanta Falcons legend.

31 Bob Whitfield: All-Pro Tackle, Media Mogul, Original Mr. Housewife of Atlanta

One thing is for sure: no one's ever said that Bob Whitfield is boring.

Coming in at 6'5" and 310 pounds of blocking fury and gregarious character, Whitfield become a beloved figure in Atlanta, thanks to his on-the-field performance and durability and his exploits away from it.

The Falcons took the hulking tackle out of Stanford back in 1992. The 21-year-old was considered one of the nation's top prospects, an unusually athletic junior lineman with incredible upper-body strength and a high football IQ. The Falcons snagged him with the eighth pick, and he wound up playing in parts of 11 games in his rookie season.

That was the last time, save his final season in red and black, that Whitfield did not start a game he was healthy for. He quickly became the closest thing to a franchise left tackle the Falcons had had in many years.

From 1993 to 1999 Whitfield played in and started every game for the Falcons. That didn't always help his reputation, as Jeff George took more than 40 sacks in a brutal 1995 campaign, and even Chris Chandler took 45 in the magical 1998 season. But Whitfield was hardly to blame for all of those miscues, and he helped pave the way for some of Jamal Anderson's best efforts.

It was that road-grade run blocking on the left side of the line that made Whitfield such a popular man in Atlanta. It's not a coincidence that Whitfield's arrival in the starting lineup coincided with Erric Pegram racking up 1,185 yards on the ground in 1993, with backup Steve Broussard averaging more than five yards per carry as well.

Whitfield did great things for Craig "Iron Head" Heyward the next two years and then Anderson after that. During his prime, there may not have been a better run-blocking left tackle in the NFL.

Whitfield also had a bit of a media mogul in him. He started Patchwerk Records in 1993, and the studio soon became a place to go for Southern hip-hop and soul artists ranging from the Goodie Mob to Bobby Brown. For years, if he wasn't on the field holding up defensive ends, he was in the studio.

As it turned out, 1998 was the defining year of his career and the underappreciated Whitfield's first and only Pro Bowl. The halo from Chris Chandler's terrific season and Jamal Anderson's 1,846-yard effort would have been enough to get him there, but these Falcons went 14–2 in the regular season and made it to the franchise's first Super Bowl. Whitfield was a huge part of making that happen.

In 1999 he missed his first game with the Falcons, starting only 15 games that season. He continued to line up at left tackle for the team for the next four seasons after that, though. During that time, the team moved on from 1998 heroes Chandler and Anderson, replacing them with exciting rookie Michael Vick and wily Warrick Dunn, one of the finest runners the Falcons have ever had.

It was only in 2003, a full 13 seasons after he was selected in the first round, that Whitfield's career with the Falcons came to a close. After restructuring his deal to stay in Atlanta, the then-32-year-old Whitfield lost some of the power that had made him such an effective blocker and then went down at midseason with a broken fibula. The Falcons released him in the 2004 preseason before injuries forced them to try to re-sign him. Stinging from the release, Whitfield said no.

It was only in this post-Falcons period that Whitfield became known for anything besides the occasional boast and his play on the field. After one season as a backup in Jacksonville, Whitfield moved on to the New York Giants, where he started nine games over the next two years. It was there that Bob Whitfield the personality became as famous as Bob Whitfield the player.

His first was a series of head-butts during games while with the Giants, which earned him the unflattering nickname "Head-butt Bob." Unfortunately, that was one of the final impressions he made in the NFL. He retired in 2007.

The second and perhaps more entertaining subplot was Whitfield's stint as the original Mr. Housewife of Atlanta. His wife Sheree Whitfield was a fixture on the show, and her husband's name came up once or twice following a very public divorce and child-support battle that has stretched on over the last few years.

It's very rare that you can say an All-Pro left tackle, unwitting reality television star, and media mogul inhabit the same body. Bob Whitfield did it all.

The Falcons Got It Right

The Falcons got it right the first time. No, not the winning. That took a while.

They got it right the first time with their first draft pick, Tommy Nobis. He was a fierce linebacker/guard out of Texas, and he was NFL Rookie of the Year in 1966 and voted to the Pro Bowl as a linebacker.

All-American Texas linebacker Tommy Nobis, left, and Rankin Smith Sr.,
owner of the Atlanta Falcons, sit down to sign Nobis' Falcons contract on
December 14, 1965.

He was signed December 14, 1965, and he became known as
"Mr. Falcon." That's getting it right the first time.

He wore No. 60, and when he came off the field to sit on the
edge of the bench, he didn't quickly throw on a hat to cover up a
mop of hair for the cameras. He got his own water and held the
cup. Nobody had to squeeze a burst into his mouth.

Look up Nobis. You will agree, the Falcons got it right the
first time. Larry Csonka, the running back for the Dolphins, said
he would rather come face to face in the hole with Dick Butkus of
the Bears than Nobis. Butkus was widely regarded as the best linebacker of the era, but to those who played the game, Nobis was on
the same high level as Butkus.

Nobis won the Outland Trophy and Maxwell Trophy at Texas. And just how many football players have been courted from outer space? Nobis was drafted by the Falcons of the NFL and Houston of the old AFL. NASA mission control, of course, is in Houston, and the Gemini Mission 7 astronaut Frank Borman transmitted back to earth, "Tell Nobis to sign with Houston."

He was voted to the NFL's All-Decade Team in the 1960s. He kept some serious company in those days on the A-list of players: Johnny Unitas and John Mackey of the Colts, Bart Starr and Paul Hornung of the Packers, Jim Brown and Leroy Kelly of the Browns, Gale Sayers and Butkus of the Bears. Think about Merlin Olsen of the Rams and Roosevelt (Rosey) Grier. Nobis was rated alongside those guys. The problem was he played for the Falcons, which may be the biggest reason he is not in the Hall of Fame.

The Falcons did not win much, but Nobis was never in a hurry to leave town. He said the fans were always terrific to him and he considered Atlanta a first-rate sports town, even if others didn't.

"People kept telling me how tough it was going to be, and I kept telling them how good the people were," Nobis said. "We were building a team from scratch, so I knew it wasn't going to be easy. I liked what I saw.

"The football fans here got to see people like Johnny Unitas and the Colts come here, and that must have been a thrill for Atlanta fans. The thrill for me was just being in the NFL and working hard and giving effort. It was a great time with the newness of it, and I was fortunate to be a part of it."

I used to see Nobis in the press box. It was obvious he was a football player. He walks to one side, probably a knee injury because of so many crackbacks. He is still thick and has a square jaw and just looks like he played the game.

The Falcons got it right the first time, indeed.

33 White Shoes

Most Falcons fans know the Dirty Bird, the dance that was a calling card of the 1998 Super Bowl team. Now, go find a clip of the Funky Chicken. It was the calling card of the punt returner Billy "White Shoes" Johnson. Talk about some fun.

It was a leg-wobbling gyration that stoked the fans and infuriated opponents. It was finished off by the splits, a behind-the-back maneuver with the football, and six points showing up on the scoreboard by the player who was named the punt returner for the NFL's 75th Anniversary Team.

Johnson played for the Falcons from 1982 to 1987. He made his name in Houston playing for the Oilers, but he is a Falcon, no doubt about it.

White Shoes made the Pro Bowl for the Falcons (1983) after a stint in the Canadian Football League and was named the 1983 NFL Comeback Player of the Year. He finished his NFL career with 3,317 punt-return yards and 2,941 yards on kick returns. He returned eight kicks for touchdowns. He also caught 337 passes for 4,211 yards.

One of his most memorable plays as a Falcon came as a receiver, not a returner, on November 20, 1983, against the 49ers. The Falcons trailed 24–21 with only seconds remaining, and they were at the San Francisco 47-yard line.

Quarterback Steve Bartkowski threw the Hail Mary down the field, and Johnson caught it at the 5, stumbled backward for a moment, but eluded two tacklers and scored with two seconds left. The Falcons won 28–24.

Here is the important stuff about Johnson. He was 5'9" and was not drafted until the 15th round. He was a Division III player

(Widener University) who ended up in the College Football Hall of Fame in 1996, which ought to say something about his character.

Johnson is from Boothwyn, Pennsylvania, and attended Chichester High School. He labeled himself "a skinny little kid," and not even his speed could get him any attention from Division I schools.

It was in high school where he first got the nickname "White Shoes" because he dyed his cleats white.

It was too bad for the Eastern programs like Penn State, Rutgers, West Virginia, Syracuse, and even Maryland down I-95. Johnson would have fit in nicely. He had 5,404 career all-purpose yards and finished with nine NCAA records and 24 school records.

The Houston Oilers took him in the 15ᵗʰ round of the 1974 draft, and off he went.

"People remember the dance," said former 49er Randy Cross, "but he was a great football player."

Bum Phillips, his coach in Houston, said Johnson made people stand up in their seats. They expected something exciting to happen from White Shoes whenever he touched the ball.

"It's your foundation," he told the *Victoria (Texas) Advocate* in 2010. "If you don't have a foundation, and you can't build up a foundation, then you're in trouble."

Johnson had speed and heart, and it cost him in 1986. He tried to stay out of the trainer's room in training camp in 1986, practicing on a sore foot, and tore a tendon in the bottom of his foot. He was coming off a 1985 season where he had 62 caught passes (a good number for that time), but he was put on injured reserved. The 4.5 speed and the moves wouldn't be the same.

White Shoes retired in 1987 at the end of a 13-year NFL career. Considering he was "a skinny little kid" and big kids were taking full-speed running shots at him on returns, he had a productive NFL career. He got further than most people thought he could, and it wasn't because of the white shoes.

34 Roddy: What the Falcons Needed

One of the complaints about Rich McKay, when he was in Tampa Bay building a Super Bowl champion, was that he did not know how to draft a quality wide receiver.

So when McKay locked on to Roddy White, a wideout from Alabama-Birmingham, there was a suspicion that McKay was about to waste a first-round draft pick. Hardly. White has simply become the top wide receiver in Falcons history, if you judge him by the statistics.

In 2011 White was named to the Pro Bowl, catching more than 100 passes for the second consecutive season, and he passed Terance Mathis for the all-time team in career yards. Mathis got his numbers in eight seasons, White in seven.

White led the NFL with 115 catches in 2010, which was also a team record. Since 2008, he has more receptions than any other receiver in the NFC.

There's more. White is just the eighth receiver in NFL history to record five consecutive seasons with 80 receptions or more.

White and Michael Jenkins were drafted as weapons for another Atlanta quarterback, Michael Vick. One was the go guy, the other the sticks guy. White could fly, Jenkins could catch the short ball and make it a successful third down.

McKay, who is now the president of the Falcons, talked about the risk/reward of drafting an explosive receiver from a small school. McKay was the general manager when White was drafted 27th overall in the 2005 draft.

"We couldn't watch more tape than we did on him," McKay said. "In the end we became convinced his athleticism was so good for his size.

Wide receiver Roddy White (84) celebrates his touchdown against the Arizona Cardinals during the first half of their matchup in Atlanta on September 19, 2010.

"We had some receivers in Tampa that hadn't worked out, so I definitely went in a little scared about drafting him. But, you know, players tend to fail if you don't stay with them. We stayed with him."

White started out looking like a bust, and it seemed nightlife came before football early in his career. It's something that happens routinely with young players: they get caught in the glare of celebrity, and they have money.

White pulled himself out of the ditch with the help of Petrino …not Bobby, the head coach, but Paul, the assistant coach.

"[Assistant coach] Paul Petrino did a good job when he was here of getting Roddy to focus on his weight and focus on his off-season," McKay said. "I think Joe Horn showed him what it took to be a pro. Also, toughness was never a problem for him."

This was a 6'1" receiver who played at a small high school in South Carolina and a non-BCS conference. There was concern he didn't have the pedigree. But White's competitiveness trumped the notion that he could not handle the rigors of the game because he had not been exposed to SEC football.

All you had to do was watch him block. The Falcons prefer to operate down the middle of the field with the run game and tight end. White helps make sure the ambitious cornerback does not get involved in run support. He is a muscular 6'1" and weighs more than 200 pounds, so there is some shock to White's block.

The Falcons have had other notable wideouts: Andre Rison and Terance Mathis, among others. Perhaps White has been helped along statistically by the consistency of quarterback Matt Ryan, but it is hard to put any other receiver in the team's history ahead of him skill-wise, even the gentleman Mathis.

White could put up big numbers for several more years. For one thing, Ryan continues to develop as a quarterback, and more of the game will be put in his hands. Michael Turner, the feature

Roddy White: By the Numbers

Put Roddy White's career stats on a piece of graph paper. It looks like he was attached to a rocket: straight up.

Bobby Petrino, the one-and-done Falcons coach in 2007, was not all bad. Neither was his brother, wide receivers coach Paul Petrino, who was probably the most respected coach in the locker room, according to White.

White had 30 catches in 2006 and then blasted off with 93 in 2007. He continued his upward trend with 88 catches in 2008. There was a downturn in 2009 to 85 catches, but the presence of Hall of Fame tight end Tony Gonzalez had something to do with that.

White then hit another level with 115 catches in 2010 and led the NFL. In 2011 he had 100 receptions and made the Pro Bowl for the fourth-straight year.

Season	G	GS	Rec	Receiving Yds	Avg	Lng	TD	Rushing Att	Yds	Avg	Lng	TD	Fumbles FUM	Lost
2011	16	16	100	1,296	13.0	43	8	--	--	--	--	--	--	--
2010	16	16	115	1,389	12.1	46	10	1	3	3.0	3	0	1	1
2009	16	16	85	1,153	13.6	90T	11	1	2	2.0	2	0	1	0
2008	16	15	88	1,382	15.7	70T	7	2	4	2.0	2	0	1	1
2007	16	15	83	1,202	14.5	69T	6	1	-2	-2.0	-2	0	3	2
2006	16	5	30	506	16.9	55	0	--	--	--	--	--	1	1
2005	16	8	29	446	15.4	54T	3	4	12	3.0	16	0	1	1
TOTAL			530	7,374	13.9	90	45	9	19	2.1	16	0	8	6

back, is toward the end of his contract, and his carries may go down from 20 per game to 15 per game. Sure, the wide receiver Julio Jones is going to get more and more involved in the passing game and start to put up numbers, but White is also going to see more single coverage as Jones becomes more visible and dangerous. Jones has also had some injury issues, which could limit his availability.

Roddy White is past the halfway point of his career, but don't be looking for a downturn in numbers just yet.

35 The Dirty Bird

Dan Reeves, who was two days shy of 55 at the time, did it. You can do it. I just can't explain to you how to do it. Thank goodness for YouTube.

The Falcons, who were on their way to the Super Bowl in 1998, had a dance: the Dirty Bird, which was part of their identity. The Dirty Bird wasn't just a statement; it was Atlanta's fling with some fun...for a change. The effervescent running back Jamal Anderson had the best Dirty Bird because it was mostly a touchdown celebration, and Anderson was in the end zone more than most Falcons.

The Dirty Bird, a flapping of the wings and a step on one foot then the other, was reported to have been created by the tight end O.J. Santiago in a 41–10 victory over the Patriots. Santiago's dance grew legs, so to speak, in Atlanta, and as the Falcons marched on that season toward the Super Bowl, there was a national audience.

The topper was the country boy Reeves doing the Dirty Bird as the Falcons were presented the trophy in Minnesota for winning the NFC Championship Game.

But nobody could do the Dirty Bird like Anderson, though. He was a California guy, full of gusto and fun inside the Falcons locker room. And he could run the rock.

Anderson played eight seasons for the Falcons and had 5,336 yards rushing. He had 156 receptions for 1,645 yard to go with it. He was not just flashy; he was a workhorse. Anderson carried the ball a then-NFL-record 410 times in 1998 as Atlanta got to its only Super Bowl.

The Falcons offense, because of Anderson, was full of play-action passes, and quarterback Chris Chandler could create indecision in the defense whenever he turned to hand the ball to Anderson or just make it a play fake and throw the ball downfield.

Anderson ran for 1,846 yards and scored 14 touchdowns for the 14–2 Falcons.

In 2001 Anderson suffered a career-ending knee injury, but there was always going to be a place for him in the game. He was a natural for TV and radio, and his spicy commentary can be heard throughout Atlanta during the season.

As for the Dirty Bird, you can still see it in the Georgia Dome during home games. The Falcons will get on a roll, and fans who remember that joyous 1998 season when Atlanta was respected by the rest of the league, will break out in the Dirty Bird.

36 Center of Attention

You want to measure loyalty to an organization? It is not just how many years a player stays in one place. It's him following the team all the way into the next generation of players and putting some money back into the organization.

Jeff Van Note retired in 1986 and still buys season tickets. The guy is part of the Falcons Ring of Honor. Somebody should be buying him tickets for 18 years of service and continued loyalty.

Van Note played in six Pro Bowls, which isn't bad for a guy drafted in the 11th round. He played in 246 games for the Falcons and started 225 of them.

He was a center, the skill position on the offensive line, which was fitting considering Van Note played college football at the University of Kentucky out of high school (in high school he played quarterback), playing running back and defensive back, and later fullback, linebacker, and then defensive end. He also played quarterback in high school. It doesn't seem possible that a man that size could play in the backfield, but Van Note had feet, as they say, and he could move those feet. That was his deal. He could move out and block people with agility and then let willpower do the rest.

Even with those nimble feet, strength, and work ethic, it took Van Note a little time to get some traction in the NFL. The Falcons let him play a game…and then cut him. He was sent packing to Huntsville and a minor league football organization.

"It was the Intercontinental Football League, and I played there eight weeks," Van Note said. "That's when I realized how much of a business it really is. It's a job, and you better approach it that way. There wasn't any movement at the time. As far as free agency, it was a myth, so you belonged to a team, unless they cut you."

Van Note still remembers flying to a game in Orlando in an old paratrooper plane. The players' backs were against the walls of the plane, and they rode down and rode back. They paid him $300 per week, or a quarter of his contract, to play for Huntsville.

Van Note tried to stay as positive as he could, even when Norm Van Brocklin, the coach, told Van Note he was going to play center in the NFL.

"It was the first day of camp, and that night I called my wife and said, 'They're moving me to center, I'll be home in a day or two,'" Van Note said. "I remember playing against Sam Huff, the linebacker from West Virginia. He made me look bad one night. Wouldn't let me hit him." Now, though, Van Note could hit who he wanted.

When his beard grew gray later in his career, Van Note looked more like a Viking, but he was a Falcon, through and through.

After a few thousand plays, Van Note retired in glory in 1986. He still lives in Atlanta and gets back home to Louisville, Kentucky, twice a month. When he was on the radio giving analysis, it was always spot-on commentary. Van Note knew exactly how to throw a cushion under a poor showing by the Birds, yet give the listeners some firm takeaway of what happened.

One thing about Van Note: when the Falcons were losing a lot of games when he was playing, he did not think about losing the next game or have a mentality that the day was done before it started. He never thought that way. He always said, "Get ready to win the next one." That's a pretty healthy outlook.

"We didn't know how to win consistently," Van Note said. "We had flashes of it, but we never put it all together. Offense, defense, special teams, front office. We had flashes at one time or another."

For a player his size, Van Note could run, so he played on special teams. He was the middle blocker on kickoff returns, among other special teams duties, and he was on the field a lot in his early seasons with the Falcons.

It was a rough-and-tumble existence in the trenches. There were head slaps and cut blocks. Players, he said, would wrap the hard tape rolls inside their forearm pads and whack offensive linemen in the head. If you didn't keep your feet moving in piles, there was a risk of a serious knee injury.

Van Note can look up at the names on the Ring of Honor and find the names of former stars he played with. He took his children to games, and they saw him on the marquee in the Georgia Dome.

"It's a source of pride, having played for the Atlanta Falcons," Van Note said. "I see my name up there, and I am thankful to all the fans and to the Falcons for putting me up there."

37 The Note: Petrino's Exit

The players kept the goodbye note from their head coach pinned to their lockers. It is usually a forbidden thing for reporters to see notes from a head coach to the players or to try and intrude on a player's space and read what's inside his stall.

This time, though, the players invited reporters to read the note from Bobby Petrino, their coach, who split town on a 3–10 team to take the head coaching job at Arkansas. Some highlighted the text in yellow. Others added some of their own dialogue: "Coward" was scrawled across the bottom of one player's copy. "Good riddance" was another jab back at Petrino. The players wanted reporters to feel some of their scorn for Petrino.

The note read:

Out of my respect for you, I am letting you know that, with a heavy heart, I resigned today as the Head Coach of the Atlanta Falcons. This decision was not easy but was made in the best interest of me and my family. While my desire would have been to finish out what has been a difficult season for us all, circumstances did not allow me to do so. I appreciate your hard work and wish you the best.

Sincerely,

Bobby Petrino.

The players scoffed. They shook their heads. They called Petrino names. *Gutless* was probably the word heard most often. In 2011, four years after he dumped them at the curb, they still call Petrino names at the team's headquarters in Flowery Branch.

It was a messy divorce. Petrino's character was questioned, and he was dogged by his abrupt departure his first season back in college football. When he appeared at the annual media gathering

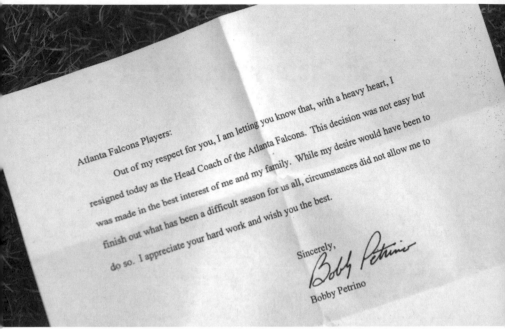

Atlanta Falcons Players:

Out of my respect for you, I am letting you know that, with a heavy heart, I resigned today as the Head Coach of the Atlanta Falcons. This decision was not easy but was made in the best interest of me and my family. While my desire would have been to finish out what has been a difficult season for us all, circumstances did not allow me to do so. I appreciate your hard work and wish you the best.

Sincerely,

Bobby Petrino

Bobby Petrino

A copy of Petrino's cowardly note, which he left with each of his players when he slunk away to take the coaching job at Arkansas.

of the Southeastern Conference coaches later in July, Petrino was greeted with questions about how he could recruit and gain trust of high school players if he would walk out on one team. Would he do it again?

A year later he was still being asked about his character. He snapped back at a reporter, "Ask Ryan Mallett about my character."

The character questions were legitimate ones. Petrino signed a five-year, $24 million contract with the Falcons when he left Louisville. There was all sorts of promise because he would pair his *X*s and *O*s with the quarterback Michael Vick. Only Vick never took a snap for Petrino. The quarterback went to prison for his role in a dogfighting ring, and the organization plummeted on the field and at the box office. All the work the Falcons had done luring fans back to the Georgia Dome was flushed.

Petrino grabbed the first ride out of town following the team's fourth consecutive loss. It was a season of decisive defeats with the four losses coming by an average of 15.4 points.

There was tension with his NFL players throughout the 2007 season as Petrino tried to impose college-like mandates on his team. He banned music on the team's bus, so before one bus ride, cornerback DeAngelo Hall arrived with a boom box the size of a refrigerator and sat in the second row behind Petrino.

In another Hall-sponsored altercation, the cornerback thought Paul Petrino questioned Hall's manhood in practice one afternoon and took a swing at the wide receivers coach, who was the brother of the head coach.

Despite that, Paul Petrino was actually admired by the Falcons wide receivers. He was a tireless worker and paid attention to detail. Roddy White, the Falcons' All-Pro wide receiver, said Petrino helped turn his career around. Paul Petrino would hunt White down late at night with phone calls to chase him out of nightclubs on the west side of Atlanta.

White missed Paul Petrino on the sideline. But, like a lot of his teammates, White did not miss Bobby. Not one bit.

38 Roddy White: Momma's Mandate

His first two seasons in the NFL, Roddy White knew the routes to the nightclubs and bars better than he knew the pass routes he was supposed to run in practices and in games. It was November 2006, and White, who had been a first-round pick, was suddenly benched. He was unreliable and seemingly unrepentant.

Then his mother became involved. White called Joenethia to tell her he had been benched. He was shamed, but nothing felt as bad as what he heard next from his mother. It was a scolding, as if he still lived with her. "Well, then," she said, "I need to pack up and move down there and take care of you like you're a baby again."

It was White's wake-up call. He did not want his mother stomping into town.

"No, no, don't do that; I got this," he told her.

He did have it. With the help of former Atlanta receivers coach Paul Petrino and a new work ethic, as well as his mother's threat, White dramatically turned his career around. He went from 30 catches in 2006 to 83 receptions in 2007.

In 2008, with rookie quarterback Matt Ryan, White caught 88 balls. In 2009 he hauled in another 85 passes and became the first receiver in Falcons history to have three seasons with at least 80 catches and 1,100 yards.

In 2010 White was elevated to the same status as the league's top receivers, the Colts' Reggie Wayne, the Cardinals' Larry Fitzgerald, and the Texans' Andre Johnson. The Falcons finished the season 13–3 with White as one of the centerpiece players on the offense.

It was a steep climb from the rookie trap he had fallen into. White was a first-round pick out of the University of Alabama-Birmingham in 2005, the 27th pick overall, and he had money for the first time. He strayed to the nightclubs and bars in Buckhead and the west side of Atlanta.

Frequently, White said his nights would end at 4:00 AM. Instead of going home and risking missing morning meetings, White would drive to the Falcons facility, punch in the code to get in the building, and sleep in the player's lounge. When he woke up, he would sit in the steam bath to rid his body of the toxins from the night before.

White had 29 catches in 2005 and 30 in 2006. He was ridiculed for dropped passes and labeled as a bust-in-progress.

"It kind of scared me, especially my second year when I didn't start anymore," White said. "I needed to get my act together because they might cut me.... I was mentally out of football at that point. Every day I showed up at the facility and just walked around, basically didn't want to do anything. I was just here."

Then the Falcons fired coach Jim Mora and hired Bobby Petrino, who brought in his brother, Paul, as the receivers coach.

"Bobby and Paul, they was like, 'You're going to be the guy. Don't worry about what other people say,'" White said. "'We're starting over, so you've got to get yourself ready.'"

In the first minicamp in May 2007, Bobby Petrino yelled for the starters to get on the field. White stood there. Paul Petrino said, "What are you doing? Get in there."

"I was like, relieved," White said. "I was back where I wanted to be. He got on my butt every day. He said, 'You need to outwork everybody.' I tried to win every drill."

Paul Petrino said that when he first worked with White, he was rolling into his routes and not sticking his foot in the ground and making firm cuts. His routes were not precise, and if the quarterback threw an accurate pass, White was out of position to make the catch.

"He dropped passes, and they said he had bad hands, but that wasn't the case," said Petrino, who is currently the offensive coordinator at Illinois. "He was just not in the right position to catch the pass. He worked hard to correct his footwork."

White, a two-time state wrestling champion in high school, learned how to better use his powerful hands to get a release off the line of scrimmage from the bump-and-run tactics of cornerbacks. He was 6'0" and weighed 211 pounds, and he would burst off the line and suddenly became hard to handle.

The Falcons started throwing more balls to White in practice, building his confidence, and there was a transformation. Football became the most important thing in his life, not the nightlife.

Petrino did something else. He treated White like a college player, because that was the coach's background at Louisville. He stayed in touch with his receiver, even after hours, and if he heard White was out carousing, Petrino would send a simple text message: "Get your butt home."

Darrell Hackney, White's best friend and his quarterback at UAB, said White's first two seasons were a struggle because of the lifestyle and the pressures of being a first-round pick.

"You know what they say—more money, more problems—and that was that," said Hackney, who lives in Atlanta. "Those first two years, there was a lot of pressure. When he dropped passes, it was eating at him. He's figured it out now.

"There are times I try to call him now in the off-season to go have lunch, and he'll say, 'Can't do it. Me and Matt Ryan are about to hit the field.'"

Pat Sullivan, the head coach at Samford University in Birmingham, was the offensive coordinator at UAB when White was there. Sullivan and his team stopped here on the way to a road game, and he had White speak to the team.

"I had heard about the first couple of years in Atlanta and how he had trouble getting on track," said Sullivan, the 1971 Heisman Trophy winner at Auburn. "Now he has the bit in his mouth and wants to succeed. He has matured so much. The way he talked to our team about priorities showed how far he has come the last couple of years."

His mother said White has calmed down, but he also knows she is just four hours away and knows the way to Atlanta. She comes to most home games with her mother and White's great-grandmother. All three wear White's No. 84 jersey in the Georgia Dome.

"I'm so proud of him," said his mother. She hesitated for a moment and then chuckled, "I knew he didn't want me coming down there."

39 Ryan: He Is the Guy

I can still remember that 2009 game against the Jets when the 6–7 Falcons were driving and needed to score. A saboteur lurked in the Jets stands.

Atlanta was down 7–3, and they really, really needed to score. You see, the Falcons were under a mandate from owner Arthur Blank. He wanted a 9–7 finish to the season so Atlanta could have back-to-back winning seasons for the first time in the franchise's history.

Blank wanted his Birds to throw that other bird, the albatross, to the ground. He made it clear in the building that week before the Jets game. So Ryan, with a hyperextended toe—which means it might as well have been broken—played the game.

He got under center on fourth down from the Jets' 6-yard line with less than two minutes to play.

Ryan dropped back and, just as his arm came up to throw the pass, a snowball landed to his left. A Jets fan in the stands had tried to time it up just right and distract the Falcons quarterback. OK, maybe not distract him, maybe hit Ryan right between the eyes as he tried to throw the pass.

The snowball missed. The pass didn't. Ryan hit Tony Gonzalez with a touchdown strike with 1:38 to play. The Falcons won 10–7. They won the next two weeks and were 9–7 and, for the first time in 43 years, had winning seasons back-to-back.

I wonder if a jumpy quarterback might have flinched and missed the window to the receiver when that snowball exploded on the turf. Ryan didn't flinch. He followed through.

Touchdown.

I asked Ryan if he saw the snowball. "No," he said.

He had to have seen something. "Nope."

Ryan was locked in. He gets that way. Through the 2011 season Ryan had taken the Falcons on 16 fourth-quarter or overtime drives to win games. That is a significant number.

He was the right pick on Draft Day 2008, and he is still the right pick. But Ryan still has work to do. Some NFL teams think he can be bothered by crowd noise. He is reluctant to stick a ball into tight corners. He is a different quarterback on the road than at home in some games.

On the other hand, Ryan can throw the bench route, that fade into the sideline. I still remember the third-down pass to Michael Jenkins that ignited a game-winning drive against the Ravens in the Georgia Dome during the 2010 season. The Ravens insisted Jenkins was out of bounds. He wasn't. Ryan dropped the throw in there.

The first time I saw Matt Ryan in person was at a Boston College game his senior season at Georgia Tech. There was a pass he threw—the same pass he threw to Jenkins. It was a deep out; he put it over the shoulder of the receiver, and the defender had no shot at it. It was a beautiful throw.

That night I was working for CBS Sportsline. I wrote that the Falcons, if they had a chance, should grab Ryan in the draft. He was the franchise quarterback to draft around. He beat Virginia Tech with a late rally; he could perform under pressure.

The Falcons picked Ryan. They had to.

The complete book of Ryan has not been written. He is 0–3 in the playoffs and has not played well in the postseason, but one has to consider how long it takes for a quarterback to bloom. Drew Brees won one playoff game his first eight seasons in the league. Eli

Manning, more highly regarded than Ryan, flubbed his first two playoff games.

There are plenty of us who do not think Ryan's third playoff calamity had as much to do with him as the failings of the offensive line. That line was inconsistent during the 2011 season, and it was clear the Falcons missed their spiritual offensive line leader, Harvey Dahl. He was the brawler who gave the Falcons their reputation.

Ryan has not reached his prime. He has something left. There is a peak to be reached, and he is not there. The important thing is that he keeps giving the Falcons chances at the Super Bowl. That means making the playoffs, and he knows how to do that.

40 Speaking of QBs: Bart

Matt Ryan is still not the best quarterback in Falcons history. Not yet anyway. Steve Bartkowski was under center for 11 years in Atlanta. He was Rookie of the Year in 1975. He is the Falcons all-time leader in passing yards with 23,470 and the franchise record holder for touchdown passes in a career with 154 and 300-yard games with 12.

Bartkowski was the quarterback when the Falcons won a playoff game. They beat Philadelphia 14–13 on Christmas Eve in 1978.

Ryan *will* win a playoff game for the Falcons. He will likely win more than one, but until he does, Bartkowski is still the boss of Falcons quarterbacks. He was there 11 years and beloved enough around town that he serves on the team's board of directors.

Bartkowski was the first pick of the 1975 draft. He was picked ahead of the Hall of Fame running back Walter Payton. If Bart's career had fizzled—if he had been a bad guy, a troublemaker—there would be a lot of scorn directed at the Falcons in hindsight: "How could you have taken this guy over Sweetness, the great Payton?"

But Bartkowski stayed in the NFL for 12 seasons. He was not a flop. He was productive. The Falcons went to the playoffs three times with Bart as the quarterback, which is how many times Ryan has gone.

Remember, Bartkowski was the NFL Rookie of the Year in 1975. He threw for 1,662 yards and 13 touchdowns. Some of the top quarterbacks in the game were in their golden years: Fran Tarkenton of the Vikings and Roger Staubach of the Cowboys. Steve Spurrier was in the NFL quarterbacking the 49ers. Kenny Stabler was in Oakland.

There were some terrific young quarterbacks, such as Bert Jones of the Colts (Baltimore). Terry Bradshaw was just getting warmed up to help the Steelers to multiple championships.

In 1980 Bartkowski threw 31 touchdown passes, which is still the club record for TD passes in a season. But his bad knees were catching up to him. He was sacked a startling 51 times in 1983, and his lack of mobility hurt the Falcons. In 1986 he started six games for the Rams before retiring.

Former Falcons receiver Wallace Francis told the *Atlanta Journal-Constitution* about Bartkowski's shining moment in the 1978 playoff win over the Eagles: the touchdown pass that won the game.

"Bart threw the ball before I got to my break," Francis said. "That's what made the play so phenomenal. He read it and was going to be hit before I made my break, so he threw it where I was supposed to be. It's just the case that I ran a decent route that time.

"The winning touchdown was a play that was called from the sideline, and Coach Bennett had communicated to Steve to stay with the pattern and for me not to read the coverage, just to make sure that I got the first down. Bartkowski overruled the call and said, 'Wallace, read it.'

"The thing that I remember most about that was the leadership of Steve and him understanding what Philadelphia was doing and having the wisdom and confidence to overrule a call that had come in from the sideline."

41 Covering Vick, Sort Of

The Falcons talked about setting up fireside chats with Michael Vick in 2005. They knew he liked to fish and maybe it would be swell if reporters could talk to Vick about fishing and life beyond football. That way, there would be a better relationship, a more casual relationship with the media.

Then we all found out about the dogs. Vick wasn't really going to Virginia to fish. He was going back to pump money and resources into a dogfighting ring.

We never really knew Vick as reporters. He was under glass, like a museum piece, treated differently than other players. Some of that was to be expected. Matt Ryan is still treated differently four years into his career. He speaks with the media twice a week during the season: on Wednesday and after games.

But Vick was really sheltered. I remember a 2005 exhibition game in Jacksonville in which he looked lousy. It was raining, but he still should have looked better five weeks into training camp. Vick ducked out the back of the locker room without talking to reporters. I followed him. He had the usual crowd of people around him, including a big guy named Bruce.

Bruce was not with the Falcons. He was a private security man. "No interviews," Bruce barked. His thick arm shot out across my path as I approached Vick. It was the second consecutive game after which Vick didn't talk to reporters. That was OK with the Falcons. They sheltered their prize and even hired a woman whose job seemed to be to keep people except the networks away from Vick.

The Falcons, under orders from coach Jim Mora, even tried to keep Vick quiet the week of a playoff game. Mora insisted Vick had too much to learn, as if this was rocket science and not football. The quarterback never quite got socialized in Atlanta.

You see him now—older, more mature—and Vick can stand up to the pressure that comes with the territory of being an NFL quarterback. Sometimes I think NFL teams just underestimate their guys. They assume they can't fend for themselves or will say something stupid. Well, they do that, but a lot is forgiven.

Vick had a hand in being hard to cover. The Falcons, in fact, asked him how much media availability he preferred. Vick, of course, wanted limited exposure. A good PR man for the Falcons, Aaron Salkin, was fired in part for pushing back on Vick and letting him know there were certain responsibilities a quarterback had in the NFL.

Vick gets it now. You can see a change. It comes with age and hard knocks. He has been put in a media vise grip in Philadelphia a few times and has come out the other side just fine. He just needed some time.

42 The Man in Black: Glanville

"Fire away." That's what you did in a Jerry Glanville interview session on the field. You fired away with questions, and then he did something. He fired back...without antiseptic, without a filter.

Jerry Glanville, "the Man in Black," poses in his office next to a James Dean cardboard standup.

I remember a time when I joined the scrum coming off the field in Suwanee. Glanville was asked about the high-priced defensive back Bruce Pickens, the 1991 first-round pick from Nebraska. The club had cut Pickens loose, and Pickens was bitter.

Glanville was bitter back. "Would have been nice if he had gotten his hands on a ball, just one ball. Did he ever touch a ball here? I don't have to look at the film."

Brett Favre was drafted by the Falcons. He missed a team photo and said he got caught behind a car wreck. Glanville retorted, "Boy, you are a car wreck."

I missed him when Glanville was sent out of town. The black hats, the shades, the belt buckles, the boots, the character, the character assassinations. He was a football coach with personality. It was fun for a while, what with the tickets being left for Elvis, but then the circus got a little stale. His head coaching record in the NFL (Houston, Atlanta) was worse than .500.

Make no mistake, he was a football coach. He was not a Hall of Famer, to be sure; his era ended in failure after a nice start. Not everybody can be Bill Belichick. But frankly, I'll take some losing over having to deal with the morose, mean-spirited New England coach.

Well, it was more than some losing. It was losing to a really bad Cincinnati team in 1993. The Falcons had a chance to make the playoffs and crashed in that game…and Jerry was done by February.

He may not have been a great head coach, but Glanville was a very defensive coach. His defenses with the Falcons as an assistant were very good.

He did some stupid things. He made a mock trophy, the California Trophy, after the Falcons won six games in 1991 over California teams. Stupid. The 49ers paid him back for that one with two routs of the Birds in 1992. The combined score was 92–17.

He drove a Craftsman Truck in racing for five years. He created a dastardly and ruthless video game that had people being sliced up by swords. Lovely.

But Jerry Glanville added some spice around here. (Think Rex Ryan.) Glanville could also coach football, which he probably didn't get enough credit for.

43 Brett: We Hardly Knew You

Jerry Glanville did not trust his quarterback. The coach said he couldn't sober up Brett Favre and that he shipped him out to Green Bay for the quarterback's own good, to a place where lights go dim at 9:00 PM.

The ridiculous part of this is that Milwaukee is not far away, and they are quite well known for their beer in Wisconsin and... well...Jerry just messed up.

Beer can be found just about anywhere, and Favre would have had to be shipped to the Himalayas to keep him off the sauce. As it was, he went to Green Bay and had a great career and the Falcons had their "Curse of the Bambino" moment. The Red Sox traded Babe Ruth and regretted it; the Falcons traded Favre and regretted it.

What kind of trouble would have ensued if the team that wanted to draft Favre had been able to get their hands on him? That was the Jets. If Atlanta was trouble for Favre, as Glanville insisted, New York would have dropped the Southern-fried quarterback on his head. Remember, it was Favre who said he didn't help his cause of staying in the South by "trying to drink up Atlanta."

Ron Wolf of the Jets wanted to take Favre in the 1991 draft, but the Falcons got him first. When Wolf went to the Packers, he traded for Favre. The truth is, coach Mike Holmgren and his offense unleashed Favre, and the beer didn't keep the pair from a championship.

Glanville had a few light moments with his rookie quarterback. For example, Favre won a $100 bet that he could throw a football into the upper deck of Atlanta–Fulton County Stadium.

"Growing up in Kiln, Mississippi, and then going to college in Hattiesburg, I think Atlanta was a little too much for him," Glanville said. "Going to Green Bay was good for him, because the town closes at 10:00."

Ken Herock drafted Favre, and the quarterback became known as the "GM's boy," which still wasn't enough to save him in Atlanta. Maybe there were one too many rascals between Glanville and Favre. There was a strong debate, and Glanville insisted the kid be traded. The legend has it that offensive coordinator June Jones broke the tie and sided with Glanville. Imagine that, siding with the head coach who made you his OC.

In any case, Favre was shipped away for a first-round draft pick, and the quarterback Chris Miller belonged to the Falcons offense. Glanville and the rest went down on a sinking ship. The Falcons, by the way, drafted a Southern Miss running back with the Favre pick.

It is still mystifying that a coach who wore all black, rode motorcycles, and raced trucks could not coexist with a quarterback who liked to stay out late at night. It doesn't make sense. Glanville and Favre were never going to be Brady and Belichick, but there seemed to be more room for harmony.

Alas, for Falcons fans, the marriage never worked.

44 Glanville's Trophy

I wonder where it is—Jerry's trophy. Anybody have a guess?

I would imagine it is at the bottom of a landfill, where it belonged in the first place. Even so, I liked Jerry Glanville for stuff like the California Trophy. He would never survive in today's NFL;

somebody would have flagged him for stunts like that. There would have been a Saints-like bounty party on the prowl if he had created something like the California Trophy for some other NFL teams of that era, such as the Steelers.

So here is the background on the trophy, which was five feet tall and made of wood and finished in gold paint. The Falcons received the trophy from a local trophy maker in 1992 and presented it to themselves. The fun-and-gun Glanville was tickled by it.

The Falcons went 6–0 against California teams in 1991. They beat the Chargers 13–10. They beat the Raiders 21–17. They beat the 49ers twice, 39–34 and 17–14, and they beat the Los Angeles Rams twice by the same score: 31–14.

Glanville was feeling good about his work. The Falcons went 10–6 in 1991 and made it to the playoffs, where they beat the Saints.

"We had to find something positive about ourselves," Glanville said, defending the tactic. "We had been playing hard but not winning. We had to find something to be proud of."

So Glanville issued a proclamation. His team was the champ of California, and he added, for good measure, "We're Texas champions from last year. We beat both the Texas teams."

So in 1992 Jerry had that trophy carted to California. We all laughed. Some players did not laugh. They knew it would stir up the 49ers. They plunked it down on the end of the bench in San Francisco. Word quickly got to the 49ers locker room before the game.

The inscription read: NFL California State Champions 1991.

"It really was kind of inflammatory," said 49ers coach George Seifert. "Word was, they were going to take a victory lap after the game and hold up the trophy."

When the Falcons carted the trophy to the bench in Candlestick Park on October 18, 1992, the 49ers became incensed. They bashed the Birds 56–17. When the 49ers came to Atlanta for their first game in the Georgia Dome, they were still angry. San Francisco won 41–3.

It was such a bad idea because the 49ers had Jerry Rice, among others. They also had the real deal as far as trophies go: Super Bowl trophies…four of them.

Glanville had left passes for Elvis at the Astrodome when he was there, and he had the gaudy belt buckle and let the players play music very loud. MC Hammer was a fixture around the team, and there was a lot of fun to be had.

But the California Trophy was one of his bad ideas. It was made worse when he held up the trophy in the pregame huddle. Glanville, the ultimate circus ringmaster, should have stuck to holding up the other team's helmet.

The 49ers let the Falcons have it, even with a comfortable lead. Seifert is typically a gentleman's coach, but he allowed the Niners to run a reverse with Jerry Rice with a 42–10 lead in the third quarter. Rice scored, and it was 49–10. The 49ers had more than 500 yards of offense by the end of the third quarter, and Seifert figured the point was made and started to pull his best players.

The loss to the 49ers pushed the Falcons to 2–5. They beat a California team the next week, the Rams, but the trophy was retired and Atlanta finished 6–10 in 1992.

The Falcons finished 6–10 in 1993. Glanville was fired and replaced by June Jones.

Where is that trophy anyway?

45 Leeman Bennett: A Playoff Win...Finally

The first thing about Leeman Bennett is he is a gentleman. The second thing about Leeman Bennett is that it took all week to prepare for his Falcons teams. The 1977 team played out of its mind with blitzes and fierce defense and electrified a city that had been labeled "Loserville" by the national media.

Then the 1978 team was as dangerous as the 1977 squad because Bennett and his coaches schemed and pushed and got every last drop of talent out of the Falcons. They went 9–7 and won the organization's first playoff game ever, a 14–13 win over the Eagles.

"The players played hard for us," Bennett said. "They gave it everything they had, and it was a great group.

"I don't know if we saw the playoffs coming or not, but the players bought into what we were trying to do, and that was the real key. Teams were still having trouble picking up our blitzes that season, just like in '77."

What was gratifying to Bennett was that rivals paid more attention to the Falcons in the off-season. They were no longer a rest stop on the schedule, a team that did not demand full attention. He heard from around the league that the Falcons were no longer a pushover.

"We worked hard to get on the list of teams that you had to prepare for and beat," Bennett said. "We did catch a lot of people by surprise in '77. With our personnel we felt like we had to attack the quarterback, that when he looked to read the field, he might have a moment to throw, and that was it. We didn't have the speed and quickness in the secondary we thought we needed to have, but we had players who played hard, and we made it work.

"Pass coverage comes down to rush plus coverage. We covered people, and then the rush got there."

The highlight for Bennett wasn't necessarily the nine-win season and the playoff victory over the Eagles. It was giving the city a pulse as far as professional sports.

The other highlight was the heart of his squad. "Our identity was we laid it on the line every Sunday," Bennett said. "You couldn't say it was this player or that player. I don't recall those things very well these days, but to single out a player specifically, I just can't do it. They all played as well as they possibly could."

When they squeaked into the postseason as a wild-card team, it looked like the Falcons' charmed season might come to an end. For three quarters on Christmas Eve in Atlanta in 1978, the Falcons went nowhere on offense. They trailed 13–0. It was a game in which they committed five turnovers, and it looked like they were not even giving themselves a chance to win. Philadelphia was in a 3–4 defense, and the Falcons rushed for just 75 yards.

Then, in the fourth quarter, quarterback Steve Bartkowski found his rhythm in the passing game. He completed four of six passes, including a 20-yarder to tight end Jim Mitchell. Then, with 1:37 left in the game, Bartkowski threw a 37-yard touchdown pass to Wallace Francis (six catches, 135 yards). The extra-point kick gave Atlanta a 14–13 lead.

The kicking game failed the Eagles, who missed an extra point and a last-ditch field goal.

The next week against the Cowboys, the roles were reversed. The Falcons had all the early momentum and then faded.

"We were ahead 20–13 at the half," Bennett said. "We had all the momentum, then lost it."

Bennett lives in Atlanta half of the year and in Jacksonville half of the year. He is a tireless promoter for the city and its place in football. He maintains a blog for the Chick-fil-A Bowl and its team selection process, and you can still find him in press boxes pumping the city.

He has reason. The city pumped him and his teams as the Falcons finally gained some traction in the NFL after a fitful first decade.

"If you wanted to single out one thing about those teams in 1977 and 1978, it was how excited the whole city got when the Falcons started winning," Bennett said. "That was the best part of it. It was totally a college football town, but the city made room for us, and we had big crowds.

"I still have people today come up to me and talk about plays and players. They bring up the games and that defense and the blitz schemes, and they talk about how hard those guys played for us."

46 Jeff vs. June: The Debacle of 1996

At first he was Curious George. We were all curious if Jeff George could manage himself and unleash the power of that arm. When the ball came out of his hands, it was a thing to behold. George came to the Falcons in 1994 and was teamed up with coach June Jones and the spread offense. Things should have been adventurous and fun.

Things were adventurous, but they were not fun. Curious George went to Furious George, and the Falcons plummeted.

The Falcons went 3–13 in 1996, one year after making the playoffs. Few teams go down the drain as quickly as the Falcons. Len Pasquarelli, one of the best NFL reporters, looked it up for the *AJC*. Since the 1970 NFL-AFL merger, there have been 236 playoff teams in nonstrike seasons. Of those, only eight (less than 4 percent) won at least six fewer games the following season.

The Falcons started the season with eight losses. Defensive end Chuck Smith said the Falcons needed a defensive-minded coach, not June Jones, and he was suspended.

George, meanwhile, found himself on the trading block. In a 33–18 loss to Philadelphia on September 22, George was benched after throwing an interception in the third quarter. He went looking for a fight with coach June Jones. The sideline rant between the two was ugly and in full view of everyone.

"We needed a spark, we needed to get something going, so I made the decision to do it," Jones said after the game of benching his starter. "What was said on the sideline is between Jeff and I. I'm glad he was upset to be taken out. I would have been too."

Management didn't think it was an OK thing to be upset, because the next day George was on the trading block. He had questioned the effectiveness of Jones' spread offense, insisting the Falcons needed a run game.

George had words for Jones, but he didn't stop there. He had words for the fans who booed and booed that day in the Dome.

"These fans have been booing for 20 years," George said. "Actually, if there had been a third-string quarterback he'd have been put in there if they'd been chanting his name.... It's always something with this franchise. When it's not me, it'll be something else."

The good news for George and the Falcons was there was not a full crowd to make the discontent even louder. There were just 40,107 fans in the Dome, which meant almost half the seats were empty. The boos echoed off the empty upper deck. There was an even smaller crowd for the final home game on December 15, when just 26,519 showed up for a game with St. Louis.

It was a stark contrast to the Christmas Eve euphoria just a year earlier, when the Falcons beat the 49ers 28–27 to earn a spot in the playoffs.

That 1996 season was not only the end of the Jeff George experiment, it was the end of the June Jones era. He was fired with two years remaining on his contract. Jones was 19–29 and left town in turmoil despite leading the Falcons to the playoffs in 1995. He did OK, though, and became the coach at Hawaii.

The Falcons named Dan Reeves as head coach for 1997. In his second season, the Falcons reached the Super Bowl. The organization left the 1996 debacle behind and moved on. That's a pretty good rebound from June and Jeff.

47 The Spike and Bike: Dimitroff Rules Roster

Thomas Dimitroff is an approachable NFL executive, if you can just find him long enough to get a minute...no, make that a second. He rules the Falcons roster with a lot of energy. The only time to catch him, I have found, is to get him when he is walking off the practice field. Other times, the PR staff says he is busy, so you have to take their word for it.

You can argue with the results produced in Dimitroff's first four seasons, until you see other NFL teams that have flailed around the last four years. Then you are somewhat content, if you are a Falcons fan. Dimitroff overhauled the roster and got rid of guys who caused issues, such as the cornerback DeAngelo Hall. The Falcons made the playoffs three out of the last four years of the new regime, and they drafted the right quarterback, Matt Ryan. He has not peaked and is still on an upward arc. They got that pick right.

Sean Weatherspoon was another pick the Falcons got right, and bringing over veteran Tony Gonzalez was another superb pickup. William Moore is going to be a star safety in the NFL. He was another Dimitroff move.

We can still debate the signing of cornerback Dunta Robinson. He managed an interception, finally, on January 2 in his last regular-season game of his first year in Atlanta. But are interceptions everything there is to being a corner?

Robinson is a fierce tackler, and in the open field he can make a play. The corner on the other side of the field, Brent Grimes, got a lot of chances to make plays on passes and grew into a Pro Bowl player. In 2010 defensive end John Abraham managed 13 sacks. Did Robinson's cover skills help some? Probably. It is a mixed view, but one thing was clear: the Falcons needed a corner desperately before the 2010 season, and they signed one of the best available.

What you need to do is have a scouting sit-down with Dimitroff. Just ask about players and their makeup and their skill-sets. The guy is decisive. He knows the players he wants for the club, and he makes moves. The 5-for-1 for Julio Jones was bold. Was it a good move? We'll know in 2012 and 2013.

"Thomas is one of the most forward-thinking guys I have ever been around," said Falcons head coach Mike Smith. "As coaches, we are always thinking week to week, and personnel guys have time-lines that are much further down the road. Thomas' forethought, in terms of personnel moves, is his strength. As a coach, you're worried about Sunday, but he is looking out for the long-term future of the organization, which is impressive. His vision on how to put this team together is the most impressive thing about him."

Dimitroff does not look like your usual GM, with his spiky hair, and he does not act like one, with his hobby of mountain biking. You try and think of another GM that bikes—most of them run, golf, or sail.

Here's how Dimitroff got the job with the Falcons: It wasn't the spikes or the bikes. It was working his way up from the basement of the NFL. It was working in Canada. It was working the small college circuit.

Finally, it was working with the NFL's premier franchise, the Patriots. You have to spot talent, and he was director of college scouting in New England from 2003 to 2007. Dimitroff was responsible for the area scouts who bring the club possible draft picks and camp invitees.

The Patriots had a 77–17 record while Dimitroff was there. Was it him? Of course not. But he knew the inner workings, and he showed he could spot talent. NFL teams do not always create their own blueprints. They borrow a little of the culture and winning mind-set from other clubs and then add their own ingredients.

Dimitroff has poured himself into the Falcons' mix and has come up with a pretty good club that will eventually challenge hard for the Super Bowl.

48 Turner's First Day on the Job

Michael Turner did not slowly work himself into the soul of the Falcons offense that first season in 2008. He didn't wait for an invitation to show he was worth the big deal. Instead, he was an immediate asset to the franchise and the guy who would help the rookie quarterback Matt Ryan settle into his new job and not have to be a savior right away.

In his first game with the Falcons, Turner set the club record for yards in a game: 220. The mark still stands. It was September 7, 2008. It was the season opener and home opener in the Georgia Dome. It was against the Lions, who were among the worst NFL teams at that time, but it was still against an NFL team.

It was Turner's first career start too, and on the Falcons' second possession he romped 66 yards for a touchdown. A backup to

San Diego's All-Pro LaDainian Tomlinson for four years, Turner quickly showed he was ready to have his own team.

Turner had 117 yards and two touchdowns by the end of the first quarter. The Lions had gone 4–0 in the preseason, but any confidence they brought into the regular season was flushed away by Turner's decisive one-cut and downhill runs. Atlanta jumped to a 21–0 lead.

Asked about breaking a record right out of the box, Turner remembered all the records Tomlinson had set in San Diego. They just happened and became a matter of course, nothering to be aimed for.

"Being around that guy and seeing him break records all the time, I always wondered what it would feel like to break a record. I didn't even know I was close to breaking the record," Turner said, "but it was something that just happened. LT told me all the time they just happened."

The game was also a coming out for a rebuilt offensive line, especially the right guard Harvey Dahl, who was to become known as a brawler. He blocked the Lions until the echo of the whistle, and he kept blocking them. The Falcons had a new feature back, Turner, but they also had a new character on the offensive line with Dahl and center Todd McClure as the linchpins.

The Falcons rushed for a franchise-record 318 yards. Jerious Norwood showed his explosiveness with the ball, but injuries derailed his career before he could fully become a complement to Turner with his speed. Norwood had 93 yards rushing on just 14 carries against Detroit.

What Turner's quick emergence did was give the Falcons an identity. This was going to be a physical, run-first operation under first-year head coach Mike Smith. It was going to be downhill runs, and Ryan was going to supplement the run game, not the other way around.

Turner also finished the regular season with 1,699 yards, which ranks third in a single season in franchise history. His 17 rushing touchdowns in 2008 were the most in franchise history.

49 Here, Hold My Monkey

Joe Curtis, who saw the very first Falcons game in 1966—and every home game since—made sure he saw one other historical Falcons game. It was on the road, and he wasn't going to miss it.

It was January 3, 2010, in Tampa and he was with his friend, Jeff Morgan. Curtis was wearing his Matt Ryan replica jersey, and he had something else with him...a stuffed monkey, and the two men had it inside their tailgate tent. They left that monkey inside the tent when they went in for the game. They were going to come back after four quarters and deal with that monkey.

You know the story. The Falcons had not had back-to-back winning seasons in their existence. It was their ball and chain through the decades, an easy needle for the Saints or Bucs fans to push in. Forget that the New Orleans and Tampa Bay rooters had plenty of pitiful teams to be teased about; the Falcons had this monkey on their back.

Atlanta was 8–7 going into that game in Tampa.

And then it was gone...the Falcons won 20–10. It set off a small celebration in Raymond James Stadium and the tossing of a defenseless stuffed monkey.

The Falcons finished 9–7. They did not make the playoffs, but there was rejoicing nonetheless. It was the first time in franchise history the Falcons had had back-to-back winning seasons (they were 11–5 in 2008). There could be ridicule heaped on the organization for other things, but never again could there be snarky comments of never being competent enough to win more than they lost in two consecutive years.

Owner Arthur Blank got a game ball after the game. Matt Ryan, the quarterback, finally could get off his injured toe and rest. He had hurt it on November 29 and then had multiple numbing shots for weeks so he could play and rid the Falcons of their curse. Ryan missed two games and then helped the Falcons win three straight to close the season. There almost was no happy ending.

The Falcons beat the Bucs on November 29 and were 6–5, but Ryan was injured. One year after making the playoffs and hoping for something better than mediocre, the Falcons were cut down by injuries, and it looked like another losing season. When Ryan went down, it looked like an 8–8 season was on the way, even with a weak schedule down the stretch.

What made matters worse for the organization is that Michael Vick came into town and finished off the Falcons in an embarrassing 34–7 rout in the Georgia Dome on December 6. The Falcons tried to win with Ryan's backup, Chris Redman, and were dumped in a badly played game. It wasn't Redman; it was the entire squad. They were 6–6, and soon they would be out of the playoff picture.

On December 13 Redman was the quarterback again and he nearly engineered an upset of the undefeated Saints. Atlanta lost 26–23 in the Georgia Dome and was 6–7.

The Falcons needed three straight wins to get rid of Joe Curtis' 44-year-old monkey.

They got the first one in New York with a late touchdown to beat the Jets 10–7. Ryan returned to the lineup, and the Falcons were 7–7.

The Falcons won again the next week in the Georgia Dome against Buffalo, 31–3. They were 8–7 and only had to beat the bad Bucs. It had become a mandate from the owner that the stigma of no back-to-back winning seasons be put to rest. It's why Ryan played when he shouldn't have played.

Coach Mike Smith admitted after the game to *Atlanta Journal-Constitution* columnist Jeff Schultz that the specter of no back-to-back winning seasons weighed on him throughout the season. He kept it to himself, but he was motivated by it week to week.

"I gained an appreciation of it the day after the season last year," Smith said. "I came into the office and saw a full-page spread of the previous teams that had winning seasons and what happened to them. I haven't told many people this. But that article is taped up on my closet door in my office. I wanted it up there so I could see it every day. But it's not something I ever spoke to the team about."

The Falcons were happy to speak about ridding themselves of the ridicule once and for all.

"This is huge for the organization," Ryan said. "I'm happy for Mr. Blank and his family…. I'm happy for all of the former players. The guys that we get to meet at practice during the off-season and during training camp. You get to meet them, and you get to see what they've gone through during their time here."

Joe Curtis still has that stuffed monkey. At some point he is going to present it to coach Mike Smith. There is a picture to go with it.

"We put the monkey on Jeff Morgan's back," Curtis said. "We're pulling that monkey off his back. To beat an archrival that day, a division rival…well…that made it even more special."

1981: The Year That Could Have Been Great

It's one thing to endure a losing season in the NFL and know that you simply aren't better than a fair amount of the other teams out there. It's another thing to know that your team has the potential to be a playoff contender, but they just can't make things work. The latter is precisely the case for the Atlanta Falcons of 1981, a team that displayed so much promise, yet at the end of the day had nothing to show for it all.

In 1980 the Falcons finished with a record of 12–4. At the time it was the best the team had ever done, and to this day it stands at the third-most-successful season the Falcons have seen in more than 40 years of play. The 1980 Falcons ranked fifth in the league in scoring, fifth in points allowed, and first in turnover ratio. Leeman Bennett and Jerry Glanville had turned things around it Atlanta, it appeared, and had finally put together an impressive season overall after beginning with so much potential with the Gritz Blitz squad of 1977.

Steve Bartkowski, William Andrews, and Buddy Curry were all back for the 1981 season, providing a solid foundation to work with on both sides of the ball. Bartkowski and Andrews always posed as a threat to put plenty of points on the board, so why should this season have been any different?

Sometimes we see teams with all sorts of talent find themselves simply unable to come away with a victory. We've seen it from the Falcons plenty of times in their history; it's just a facet of the game. Things won't always go your way. Unfortunately, "things never go your way" should have been the motto for the 1981 ballclub. The team that scored the second-most points in the history of Atlanta (to this day) finished at 7–9 for the year, but a closer look at the schedule will quickly prove it could have been an entirely different season if a few things had gone their way.

The Falcons opened up the season with an absolute throttling of the New Orleans Saints. Bartkowski threw for 154 yards and three touchdowns, Andrews ran for 86 yards, and the defense hardly moved an inch. At the end of the day the Falcons came away with a 27–0 victory and a great start to the year.

Week 2 called for a little more urgency from Atlanta, as the Falcons found themselves trailing the Green Bay Packers 17–0 through three quarters. Bartkowski's four interceptions certainly did not help their case for a 2–0 record, but he and the offense managed to completely turn things around in the fourth. Glanville revved up his defense, and they locked down the Packers the rest of the way. The Falcons managed to score four touchdowns and a field goal in that last quarter of play, giving them a 31–17 win and a spotless record as of that point. If they could come back from a 17–0 deficit in just nine minutes, as the record books point out, what could possibly hold them back from making the playoffs for the second consecutive year?

In Week 3 the Falcons defeated divisional foe San Francisco, a team that would wind up winning it all that season, 34–17. Their record sat at 3–0, and that 12–4 mark from the previous year appeared as if it wasn't even going to be able to hold a flame to 1981.

About that time, the wheels started to come off for the Falcons. Despite a solid victory over a prestigious ballclub, the Falcons took several hits during the game against San Fran. The team lost three starters within five minutes of each other. Defensive end Jeff Merrow, tackle Warren Bryant, and linebacker Joel Williams all went down, creating more adverse conditions for the team going forward.

They suffered their first defeat of the season at the hands of the Cleveland Browns the following week. After losing 28–17 on the road, they traveled to Philadelphia. The Eagles then handed them a 16–13 loss, marking two straight for Atlanta. Defeats of the slimmest margins would become a habitual condition for the Falcons and the overall theme for the 1981 season.

It would be nice to say they turned things around from that point on, but of course that would be a blatant diversion from the truth. At 3–2 Atlanta traveled home to face the Los Angeles Rams. Once again the Falcons couldn't finish off their opponent, and the Rams came out with a 37–35 win. Two losses in a row by a mere five points did not sit well with anyone. This team and its supporters knew they were capable of much more.

A 41–20 victory for Atlanta over St. Louis in Week 7 spurred a little bit of promise, but it proved to be a fleeting bright spot. The ballclub reverted back to its old ways from a few weeks prior shortly after defeating the Cardinals. Week 8 was just another game that easily could have gone in their favor, yet the New York Giants managed to beat the Falcons by only three points.

The Falcons suffered five more losses after Week 8, losing 17–14, 34–20, 24–23, 21–16, and 30–28. Aside from the 34–20 loss to Pittsburgh, the team realistically could have pulled off any of the other matchups in which they were defeated. When the season came to a close, Atlanta saw seven defeats of five or fewer points, totaling 19 points in all. Seven games lost by a total margin of 19 points. A statistic like that is a clear indication of just how different 1981 could have been.

Seven Falcons were named to the Pro Bowl that season, another sign of how much talent the team truly possessed. Atlanta scored 52 touchdowns and gained 5,664 total yards in 1981, which both stand as the second-most in franchise history. Bartkowski's 30 touchdown passes were just one shy of his record-setting mark of 1980. Several individual records were set in Atlanta that season, but none of it mattered in the end. At 7–9 the team had taken a huge step backward from the year before. One has to wonder, though, how good the 1981 team could have been if just a few of those close contests had gone the other way.

51 1978: Atlanta's First Playoff Run

The 1978 seasons started ominously for the Atlanta Falcons. With four losses in their first six games, the Falcons looked like a team that would fail, yet again, to make the playoffs. Atlanta had played the 12 prior seasons without a playoff appearance, and the fans wanted to taste postseason play.

Starting in Week 7, the Falcons went on a five-game winning streak, taking their record from 2–4 to 7–4. Over the next four weeks Atlanta went 2–2 and sat at 9–6 heading into the final week of play in the 1978 regular season.

Instead of settling matters on the field, the Falcons didn't even have to lace up their cleats to earn their first-ever playoff spot in Week 16.

On Saturday, December 16, the Washington Redskins lost 14–10 to the Chicago Bears. This loss, on Atlanta's day off, pushed the Falcons into the playoffs.

On the next day Atlanta was given further assistance. When the Los Angeles Rams beat the Green Bay Packers on December 17, it gave Atlanta home-field advantage in the first week of the playoffs.

Without even taking the field in Week 16, Atlanta had earned its first-ever postseason berth and a home game. It was a good thing Atlanta didn't need to step onto the field. Because when the team did play, the Falcons lost 42–21 to the St. Louis Cardinals.

Falcons Playoff History

The Atlanta Falcons have qualified for postseason play 11 times in their 45-year history. The team first qualified for the playoffs after the 1978 season and has a 6–11 record.

Atlanta has been to the NFC Championship Game twice (1998 and 2004) and the Super Bowl once (1998).

2011 Playoffs

Wild Card	January 8	L	@ New York Giants	24–2

2010 Playoffs

Division	January 15	L	Green Bay Packers	48–21

2008 Playoffs

Wild Card	January 3	L	@ Arizona Cardinals	30–24

2004 Playoffs

Division	January 15	W	St. Louis Rams	47–17
Conference Championship	January 23	L	@ Philadelphia Eagles	27–10

2002 Playoffs

Wild Card	January 4	W	@ Green Bay Packers	27–7
Division	January 11	L	@ Philadelphia Eagles	20–6

1998 Playoffs

Division	January 9	W	San Francisco 49ers	20–18
Conference Championship	January 17	W (OT)	@ Minnesota Vikings	30–27
Super Bowl	January 31	L	Denver Broncos	34–19

1995 Playoffs

Wild Card	December 31	L	@ Green Bay Packers	37–20

1991 Playoffs

Wild Card	December 28	W	@ New Orleans Saints	27–20
Division	January 4	L	@ Washington Redskins	24–7

1982 Playoffs

Wild Card	January 9	L	@ Minnesota Vikings	30–24

1980 Playoffs

Division	January 4	L	Dallas Cowboys	30–27

1978 Playoffs

Wild Card	December 24	W	Philadelphia Eagles	14–13
Division	December 30	L	@ Dallas Cowboys	27–20

The Falcons backed into their first playoff appearance in franchise history, but it didn't matter. Atlanta was hosting a playoff game, an NFC wild-card matchup against the Philadelphia Eagles.

On Christmas Eve 1978, with five minutes to play, the Falcons were in a 13–0 hole in their first playoff game ever. Quarterback Steve Bartkowski then led his team in some holiday magic.

Bartkowski threw two touchdown passes in the final five minutes to win the game 14–13 for Atlanta. The Eagles' Mike Michel missed a 33-yard field goal with 13 seconds to play as Atlanta dodged another bullet.

The Falcons didn't fare as well in the divisional round the next week in Dallas. Atlanta led the Cowboys 20–13 at halftime but failed to score in the second half. As the Falcons watched backup Dallas quarterback Danny White orchestrate two second-half touchdown drives, they also saw their season end.

The Falcons were bounced from their first playoff run before the NFC Championship Game. But at least they had gotten some playoff experience.

52 Want to Succeed in Atlanta as a Wide Receiver? Wear No. 84

The Atlanta Falcons do not officially retire jersey numbers of the most heralded players to ever set foot on the field, but they certainly recognize greatness when it is achieved. Several athletes have made the Falcons Ring of Honor and now have their jerseys hanging in the rafters. One number that may be up there someday is No. 84. It currently belongs to one of the best Falcons wide receivers in franchise history, Roddy White, but he is not the only Falcon to don that jersey and attain greatness.

In the course of Atlanta's history there have been 13 players, wide receivers and tight ends, who have competed with the No. 84 on their back. Vern Burke was the first ever to wear it when the team started up in 1966. He was far from a superstar, but he had it first.

The first to bring prominence to this jersey was Alfred Jenkins, a hometown guy who had spent the majority of his life in Georgia. Jenkins was born in Hogansville, Georgia, and he attended college at Morris Brown, located in the very city in which he would put on some of his best performances as a pro.

After playing for the Birmingham Americans in 1974 as part of the World Football League, Jenkins was named to the All-WFL team that year. The following season he made his way back to his roots, suiting up for the Atlanta Falcons and sporting the No. 84.

In his first three years with the team, Jenkins accounted for 118 receptions for 2,154 yards and 16 touchdowns. He was steadily making an impact each year in the passing game. Jenkins missed almost the entire season in 1978, but he was back to business the following year, finishing with 50 catches for 858 yards. The next two seasons really made that No. 84 stand out in everyone's minds, as Jenkins was named to the Pro Bowl in 1980 and 1981. He was an All-Pro in 1981, and his 70 receptions, 1,358 yards, and 13 touchdowns grabbed the attention of fans and coaches nationwide.

His numbers and playing time declined over his final two seasons with the Falcons, but his name was forever stamped in the record books in Atlanta. Jenkins still ranks toward the top of the list in several statistical categories, including fourth all-time in receptions and touchdown catches for the Falcons. This was not the end of No. 84, though. The jersey's legacy carried on and later became a superstar of not only the franchise but the entire league.

Shawn Jefferson played 13 years in the NFL, and even though he only spent three of them with Atlanta, he did the No. 84 proud during his brief tenure. In 2000, his first year with the Falcons, Jefferson caught 60 passes for 822 yards. His numbers dropped off marginally the next two years, but he kept the No. 84 jersey warm for a little while until its current owner came to town.

Sharod Lamor White (better known as Roddy) was drafted by the Falcons in the first round of the 2005 NFL Draft. The franchise was in need of someone who could step up and make plays downfield, and time would come to prove that they found their man.

White's first two years in the league weren't anything to really write home about. Michael Vick only completed around 200 passes in 2005 and 2006, so White didn't exactly have the opportunity to build up his résumé too much. Things changed, though, and it didn't take long before White was recognized as an elite receiver in the NFL, feared by opposing defenses everywhere.

No. 84 was making the Falcons proud again in 2007, as White exploded for 83 catches and 1,202 yards. His breakout performance was certainly no fluke, as he posted 80-plus receptions in each of the following two seasons. After making the NFC Pro Bowl roster in 2008, the trend continued and basically became a given each year he played. To date White has made the Pro Bowl in four consecutive seasons.

In 2010 White had a record-breaking year, as he caught 115 passes for 1,389 yards, both Falcons franchise records. And 2011 was another outstanding season for the veteran, with White finishing at 100 receptions and 1,296 yards. He currently sits at 530 catches, 7,374 yards, and 45 touchdowns for his career. He already holds several team records and should break Terance Mathis' record for most passes caught as a Falcon within the next two seasons.

Needless to say, No. 84 has become one of the biggest numbers in all of Atlanta sports. You can't go anywhere in the city on game day without seeing White's number on the backs of Falcons fans. He has one of the most popular jerseys in the area and is an icon in the state of Georgia, as well as the NFL. The No. 84 jersey sits at the pinnacle of its success here in Atlanta, and it will be forever known in hearts of Falcons fans. The Falcons do not officially retire jersey numbers, but it will be a long time before another player puts on the likes of this number.

53 Claude Humphrey: Sack Master

Every NFL franchise has its fair share of NFL legends, no matter how long the team has been around. The Atlanta Falcons have been operating since 1966, and there have certainly been a number of athletes who have achieved greatness while wearing the red and black. One of the most outstanding players to ever set foot in Atlanta–Fulton County Stadium (or any stadium, for that matter) was discovered early in the beginning stages of the franchise. Claude Humphrey, a sack master extraordinaire and an Eighth Wonder of the World to the Falcons, came to Atlanta in 1968, and his name will never be forgotten around the city or in the entire NFL.

Humphrey was born in Memphis, Tennessee. He didn't venture far when he went off to college, attending Tennessee State University in Nashville. At 6'4" and 252 pounds, he was a perfect fit to play football, but *play* isn't quite the word people would use to describe what he did on the field. *Dominate*, something he did often, might be a better verb to use when telling the tales of his success assailing opposing quarterbacks.

In 1967 Humphrey took home All-American honors for his senior year with the Tigers, and it set him on a path for further greatness. No team can deny a tenacious pass rusher when they see one, and Atlanta jumped at the opportunity to select Humphrey in the 1968 NFL Draft. He was taken third overall, setting the bar relatively high for his playing career going forward.

It took no time at all to see value out of their first-round pick, as the Falcons watched Humphrey tear apart defenses the minute he became a pro. The young defensive end was named NFL Defensive Rookie of the Year in his first season, the first of many more honors to be thrown his way.

From his initial Rookie of the Year selection, his career simply skyrocketed. After three seasons in the pros, Humphrey received his first Pro Bowl selection in 1970. This spurred a trend that continued for the next four seasons. Five consecutive Pro Bowls is nothing short of spectacular. He was a physical, hardworking player who helped jump-start the franchise's defense.

With Humphrey's help the Falcons achieved their first winning record in 1971, finishing 7–6–1. That same year he was named a first-team All-Pro, another honor he went on to receive five times in his career.

After such a stellar beginning to his playing days, Humphrey suffered a knee injury that cost him the entire 1975 season. Fortunately for Atlanta he was back to his old ways in 1976, this time finishing the season with a career-high 15.5 sacks. For his efforts he was named the team's Most Valuable Player that year.

The historic 1977 defense was just another fabled addition to Humphrey's legacy. The Falcons' infamous Gritz Blitz defense marked one of the most celebrated seasons in Atlanta history, and Humphrey was right in the middle of it all. Led by defensive coordinator Jerry Glanville, the Falcons set an NFL record for allowing the fewest points in a 14-game season. They allowed just 129 points and 231.6 yards per game that year, marking some of the most significant statistics in the deep chronicles of football. Humphrey was named a Pro Bowler and an All-Pro that season.

In 1978 he helped boost the Falcons to their first-ever playoff appearance. Seriously, what else could one man do for a new team?

Unfortunately this was the last season he ever appeared in an Atlanta uniform, as he finished the final three years of his career in Philadelphia.

Humphrey finished in Atlanta with a total of 94.5 sacks, ranking him as the franchise's all-time leader in this category. He was inducted into the Georgia Sports Hall of Fame in 2004, and he was a finalist for the Pro Football Hall of Fame in multiple years, although he never quite achieved that final passage. Humphrey even made a guest appearance on an episode of *The Dukes of Hazzard*, sparking the question, "How much more Georgian can you get?"

In 2008 the Falcons placed Humphrey in their Ring of Honor, forever instilling his legendary career into the realm of Atlanta history. He was a foundation for the opening era of the Falcons history, and he will forever be remembered as one of the supreme rulers in the art of tossing quarterbacks to the ground.

54 Eat Like an All-Pro

There's a reason Tony Gonzalez, signed by the Falcons in 2009, has been ageless throughout his illustrious Hall of Fame career.

Halfway into his career, Gonzalez teamed up with Kansas City nutritionist Mitzi Dulan to change his eating habits. His diet became organic-based as he began abstaining from the convenient fast-food options that line many streets throughout this nation.

In 2007 Gonzalez briefly chose to be a vegan but didn't consume enough protein to keep his muscle mass where it needed to be to play football. Gonzalez ultimately decided to eat meat again, but will only buy free-range birds and grass-fed beef. He's even stated he's considering becoming a vegan again once his playing days are over. He was influenced by *The China Study*, written by T. Colin Campbell, which looked at nutrition and how modern food sources have impacted long-term health factors across the globe.

Gonzalez firmly believes the human body gets the most in an athletic setting by eating nutrient-rich foods free of additives.

"My body feels so much better," Gonzalez said in 2010. "When you keep things all-natural, your body responds to it, and you feel better for it. Stay away from processed food, stay away from junk food. Start supplementing correctly with natural sugar, grass-fed whey, the way it's supposed to be."

Just a couple of weeks into his first training camp with Atlanta in 2009, and after his first 12 seasons in Kansas City, Gonzalez published his own book, *The All-Pro Diet*. Gonzalez's book details his regimen of keeping animal protein intake low and organic plant-based protein high. Gonzalez claims that once he made the switch, his stamina went up and he was able to perform at a higher level, while other NFL players' careers began to fade.

"I know for sure, and I'm positive, that I wouldn't be able to sit here and talk about [my career] and playing at the level that I am without [having switched] my diet like that," Gonzalez said.

After Gonzalez began "eating clean," as he puts it, he started searching for all-natural supplements free of unneeded chemicals and preservatives. This led him to found his own company, All-Pro Science, which creates nutritional supplements for athletes. Two of his top products are a grass-fed whey protein powder and a veggie protein powder—the latter containing proteins from three different plants. Gonzalez said by blending the plant proteins together, it's easier for protein synthesis to become more potent after ingestion.

Gonzalez's impact was immediately felt when he signed with Atlanta as a free agent in 2009. In his first game as a Falcon, he hauled in five catches for 73 yards and a touchdown against Miami in a 19–7 win. He followed that up with 71 yards and another touchdown in Atlanta's 28–20 win against Carolina the following week. In his first season with Atlanta, which saw the Falcons record back-to-back winning seasons for the first time in franchise history, Gonzalez recorded 867 yards and six touchdowns.

He followed that with 656 yards and six touchdowns in 2010 and 875 touchdowns and seven touchdowns in 2011—proving he still ranks among the better tight ends in the NFL.

Entering the 2012 season, Gonzalez had amassed 13,338 yards in 15 NFL seasons. These numbers placed him first among tight ends and 11th all-time in receiving yards among all NFL players.

One of the No. 1 factors keeping Gonzalez in the game is his desire to win a Super Bowl championship. He left Kansas City for Atlanta because he felt the nucleus the Falcons were building best suited his desire to win a title before his playing days end. So far, Gonzalez has lost playoff games in 2010 and 2011 with Atlanta. Gonzalez, from his rookie season in 1997 through 2012, has never won a playoff game.

He's an optimist, though, and believes it will eventually happen. It seems time would be running out, as 2012 will be Gonzalez's 16th NFL season (he signed a two-year, $12.65 million deal after 2011). But considering the way he eats and trains, his performance on the field may not see much of a decline. At this rate, Gonzalez might still be playing when he's 40.

Quarterback Bob Berry: First 300-Yard Passer

The notion of a 300-yard passer being a big deal in the NFL today is preposterous. With the game ever evolving into a passing league that's beginning to devalue the running back, it goes to show how important having a great quarterback is.

Heading into the 1970 season, Atlanta didn't know much about what having a great quarterback who could sling the ball around to its receivers was all about. Sure, the elite quarterbacks had the occasional 300-yard game. But it wasn't as common as it is now, as evidenced by three quarterbacks topping the 5,000-yard barrier in 2011 (Drew Brees, Tom Brady, and Matthew Stafford).

In its first four seasons, Atlanta had some paltry games throwing the ball. In the 1969 season finale against Minnesota, quarterback Bob Berry threw only 13 passes, completing six of them for 70 yards. Atlanta ended up winning that game 10–3. Not too many teams could win a game today with a quarterback without surpassing the 50 percent completion mark, and for less than 100 yards.

Berry was originally drafted by Philadelphia in the 11th round but signed with Minnesota in 1965. He became a Falcon prior to the 1968 season. In the organization's first four years of existence, Berry posted the best passing game of any quarterback, throwing for 282 yards and three touchdowns against the Steelers, albeit in a 41–21 loss.

In the 1970 opener, Berry completed 11 of 20 passes for 133 yards, a touchdown, and an interception in a 14–3 Falcons win over New Orleans. The Saints defense kept Berry's Falcons from moving the ball much until the fourth quarter, when Atlanta scored both of its touchdowns.

In the following week's game, on September 27, 1970, the Falcons were forced to air out the ball against a Packers squad that jumped out to a 13–0 lead. Berry ended up throwing 44 passes, something that wasn't too common in that era. He connected on 28 of those passes for 302 yards—becoming the first Falcons quarterback to notch a 300-yard game passing. Berry's first touchdown pass of the game came in the fourth quarter and was thrown to running back Harmon Wages to cut Green Bay's lead to 20–17.

Berry followed that possession with an 18-yard touchdown toss to receiver Todd Snyder to put Atlanta up 24–20.

But it wasn't enough for the Falcons, as Carroll Dale caught an 89-yard touchdown pass from Packers backup quarterback Don Horn, which gave Green Bay a 27–24 win. Berry was the star of the day but didn't have the play that stood out, as Horn's pass traveled 56 yards through the air and just missed being intercepted by Falcons cornerback Ken Reaves. For Horn, it was his only completion in eight attempts that afternoon.

Berry played with the Falcons through the 1972 season before heading back to the team he originally signed with: Minnesota. Though he was a starter in Atlanta, he backed up Hall of Fame quarterback Fran Tarkenton when he went back to the Vikings. Berry made his only Pro Bowl appearance with Atlanta in 1969. He finished his career with 9,179 yards, 64 touchdowns, and 64 interceptions. Of his career yardage total, 8,489 yards were with the Falcons. Berry also became the first Atlanta quarterback to throw for 2,000 yards in a season as he finished 1971 with 2,005 yards. He bested that mark with 2,158 yards in 1972, his final season with the Falcons.

56 Tony Gonzalez vs. Jim Mitchell for Greatest Falcons Tight End

It's tough to debate who the better overall tight end is between Tony Gonzalez and Jim Mitchell. Though Mitchell has long held the distinction as the greatest tight end to play for the Falcons, Gonzalez may go down as the best tight end in NFL history, who happened to join the Falcons late in his career. Despite the fact that

Gonzalez signed with Atlanta in 2009, he'll forever be remembered more for his years in Kansas City.

But it's not as if Gonzalez's accomplishments in Atlanta don't put him in the conversation. A lot of what determines whether a player at a certain position is the best is the kind of value he brings. In that scenario, Gonzalez is certainly in the top two of this discussion.

In 2008, the year before Gonzalez signed with Atlanta, Falcons tight ends combined for just 211 yards. It was clear Atlanta was missing a big pass-catching target in the middle of the field who could also block effectively in the running game. Gonzalez was the first of his kind when he entered the NFL in 1997. Gonzalez possesses the skills of a wide receiver in a tight end's body. Tight ends such as New England's Rob Gronkowski and New Orleans' Jimmy Graham owe a lot of their success to how Gonzalez changed the game and the perception of the position.

In Gonzalez's first year in Atlanta, his impact was immediately felt. He was second on the team in receptions with 83 for 867 yards and six touchdowns. The Falcons finished 9–7 in 2009 but didn't reach the playoffs. In Gonzalez's second year with Atlanta, the Falcons were able to reach the postseason by claiming the NFC's No. 1 overall seed with a 13–3 regular-season record. Gonzalez's numbers dipped to 70 receptions for 656 yards and six touchdowns, though teams began bracketing Gonzalez in an attempt to take away what they saw as the most important threat in Atlanta's passing game. This allowed receiver Roddy White to work mostly in man coverage and catch 115 passes for 1,389 yards and 10 touchdowns. In 2011 Gonzalez had his best season statistically with Atlanta, hauling in 80 passes for 875 yards and seven touchdowns. Atlanta reached the playoffs for the second consecutive season but fell to the New York Giants in the wild-card round.

In his first three seasons with Atlanta, Gonzalez recorded 233 catches for 2,398 yards and 19 touchdowns. In this short time span, Gonzalez has already notched the third-most receiving yards for a tight end in Falcons history. Ahead of him in second place is Alge Crumpler, who had 4,212 yards and 35 touchdowns (most among Falcons tight ends), who played for Atlanta from 2001 to 2007.

Checking in at first place in receiving yards among tight ends in Falcons history is Mitchell, who reeled in 305 catches for 4,358 yards and 28 touchdowns during his 11-year NFL career, with every one of those years spent with Atlanta. Though Mitchell never had a receiving year quite like Gonzalez ever had, he was consistently steady in the passing game. Mitchell's best year receiving came in 1970, his second season in the NFL. He caught 44 passes for 650 yards and six touchdowns. More than a receiving option, Mitchell was known for his brutal blocking. Former linebacker Tommy Nobis once said Mitchell would routinely win weekly big-hit awards, despite being a member of the offense.

This bruising mentality led him to receive the occasional carry early in his career as he totaled 187 rushing yards with one touchdown scored on the ground. Mitchell made the Pro Bowl as a rookie in 1969 and again in 1972. Mitchell, known to never back down from a fight, infamously got into a punching bout with teammate Art Malone during a game against the San Francisco 49ers in 1973. When his playing days were over, Mitchell stayed in Atlanta and helped coach football at Morehouse College and Morris Brown College. Mitchell suffered a heart attack and passed away at the age of 60 in 2007.

It comes down to preference when debating whether Gonzalez or Mitchell is the better Falcons tight end. An old-school Falcons fan may argue in favor of Mitchell, considering he played every NFL season with Atlanta and still holds the tight end receiving yardage record. A newer-age fan could argue Gonzalez deserves the distinction due to what he's been able to bring to the offense after deciding to leave Kansas City to chase an elusive playoff victory. The devil's advocate fan may deny both and toss in Crumpler's name, considering he was former Falcons quarterback Michael Vick's top overall receiving option in the early to mid-2000s.

You can't go wrong with either decision, whether it's Mitchell or Gonzalez, or even Crumpler. Each tight end brought something unique to the table while dedicating their time to winning football games in Atlanta.

57 Visit the Hall of Fame and Find Deion's Bandana

Compared to most NFL teams, the Atlanta Falcons have a short 46-year history. Because of the brevity of Atlanta's existence, it's not unusual for the team to have only a few members in the Pro Football Hall of Fame in Canton, Ohio.

The Falcons have four former players in the Hall of Fame, and only one made what the Hall of Fame calls a "major part of their primary contribution" to the Falcons.

The three players in the Hall of Fame who spent some time with the Falcons are running back Eric Dickerson (1993), defensive end Chris Doleman (1994–95), and wide receiver Tommy McDonald (1967).

Only cornerback Deion Sanders, who spent five seasons in Atlanta, from 1989 to 1993, is listed as a primary Falcons contributor in the Hall of Fame.

Sanders was enshrined into the Hall of Fame on August 6, 2011, and gave a very emotional and heartfelt acceptance speech in which he thanked 112 different people.

Deion Sanders and his bandana-wearing bust at his Hall of Fame induction on August 6, 2011.

He told a story during that speech of how he was ashamed that his mother worked as a hospital custodian as he was growing up and that he lied about it to friends. He told the honest truth about neglecting his family and ruining relationships during the makings of his Hall of Fame career.

But as electrifying as his acceptance speech was, the one act that most will remember from his enshrinement had to deal with Sanders' trademark bandana.

Once Sanders was done thanking as many people as he could think of, he turned around to look at his bust and said, "I got one final thing because I like him, but something's missing." Sanders had a prop, and he would have received a hefty fine from the league had he been on the playing field, but no one flagged the former cornerback for this.

Sanders pulled a bandana from his new gold jacket and placed it on his bust.

According to the Hall of Fame, a volunteer assigned to get Sanders' bust to Canton asked what he should do with the bandana. Hall of Fame registrar Christy Davis took the bandana from Sanders' bust and relocated the headpiece to a different area within the Hall.

Sanders was able to get his bandana into the Hall of Fame in Canton. Now Falcons fans just have to explore a little bit to find it.

58 1973: Two Big Wins to Put Atlanta on the Map

The 1973 season was the Atlanta Falcons' eighth as a franchise. In the prior seven seasons the Falcons compiled a 30–64 record and never enjoyed a winning season. But 1973 was different, and it started in a huge way.

Atlanta went on the road to start the 1973 season, traveling to New Orleans to play the Saints. In what would turn out to be the biggest offensive output in Atlanta's franchise history, the Falcons scored 62 points and beat the Saints 62–7.

According to Atlanta Falcons historical data, the team set 35 franchise records on that first Sunday of the season. The biggest, and most obvious, is the 62 points the team put on the scoreboard.

In the 98 games prior, the Falcons had only scored more than 30 points nine times, and the team had only eclipsed 40 points twice. On that day Atlanta scored 14 points more than it ever had and won by 55 points, the largest margin of victory every enjoyed by a Falcons team.

Quarterback Dick Shiner led the way by throwing three touchdown passes, two to wide receiver Ken Burrow. Shiner threw for 227 yards on 13 of 15 passes, 64 of those yards to Burrow and 111 yards to tight end Jim Mitchell.

Shiner, starring on that Sunday, was not just surprising considering the fact that Atlanta had never seen such an offensive feat. Shiner didn't even know he was going to be the starter until the week prior, according to Associated Press accounts.

Head coach Norm Van Brocklin tapped Shiner as the starter after spending the prior year on Atlanta's taxi squad. Shiner beat out Bob Lee and Pat Sullivan during the Falcons' exhibition play to earn the starting role.

Most of the Saints crowd that day left in the fourth quarter, expecting a much better game.

Van Brocklin was expecting a better game too. "We were expecting a tougher game," said the coach after the shellacking. "Certainly we didn't expect anything like this. We thought it would be close."

It turns out that not only was it Atlanta's largest margin of victory ever, it was also the worst beating a New Orleans team had ever taken.

But while the offensive output in Week 1 was surprising, it wasn't the most exciting win of the 1973 season for the Falcons. After Atlanta beat New Orleans in Week 1, it lost its next three games. But then, starting in Week 5 on October 14, the Falcons started winning.

Atlanta's win streak was up to five games when it welcomed the undefeated Minnesota Vikings (9–0) to Atlanta on November 19. Minnesota had already clinched a playoff berth, its fifth NFC Central division title in six years. Atlanta was still gunning for its first playoff appearance and was one game behind the Los Angeles Rams in the NFC West.

Atlanta was inspired, possibly driven into a frenzy, by the 56,519 rabid fans there to watch the game. A scoreless first quarter gave way to a second where the Falcons offense posted 17 points on the scoreboard.

The Falcons scored first with a field goal, but then Fran Tarkenton connected on a Vikings touchdown pass to John Gilliam to take the lead. Then everything else in the first half went Atlanta's way.

The Falcons outgained Minnesota in yardage, 275–105, and allowed the Vikings just 13 yards on the ground in the first half. Atlanta could only manage three second-half points and had to hold off a late rally where Tarkenton threw another touchdown pass, but the Falcons did hold.

Atlanta's 20–14 win was its sixth in a row and kept their playoff hopes alive. And for the capacity crowd in attendance and Falcons fans at home watching the nationally televised game, it was the most exciting game of the season.

The Falcons eventually missed the playoffs by one game in 1973 but enjoyed their first nine-win season at 9–5. Those two games—a record-setting offensive blasting of New Orleans and a beatdown of the top team in the NFC on national television—gave the Atlanta Falcons a taste of what success could feel like.

59 Watch *Live from the D-Block*

Of the questions Atlanta Falcons video services coordinator Matt Moore gets asked frequently, the most frequent is, "How are the players to deal with? What is this guy like? What is that guy like?"

So prior to the 2005 season, Moore decided the team needed something to show off its players to the world.

The team tried rookie diaries. The project went "OK."

Then Fred McCrary happened.

McCrary came to Atlanta at the tail end of the 2004 season, and Moore said the fullback was hilarious.

"It was funny because [quarterback] Mike Vick was kind of to himself, but when Fred was around, you were like, 'Wow, this backup fullback can bring Mike Vick out of his shell.'"

Moore wished that fans could see that happening.

The next season, *The Freddie Mac Show* was born.

"Player shows, you've gotta do one," said Moore. "The fans love it because they kind of get an inside look."

And *The Freddie Mac Show* took off. The webisodes were well received, and Moore said that to this day people still stop him and ask if there are copies of old shows that they can download.

After McCrary moved on from the Falcons, the team tried other player shows with limited success. Erik Coleman stepped in and produced *Rollin' with Coleman* for a season, but since he left the team soon thereafter, that show gained little traction.

Moore and new media producer Jay Adams were brainstorming prior to the 2011 season, trying to come up with a new player show that could really sizzle.

Moore thought out loud, "What draws me when I'm in the locker room? It's where the linebackers are. The linebackers, everyone comes to them, they draw the whole locker room—whether it's [quarterback] Matt Ryan, whether it's [defensive end John] Abraham, the linemen, they all get drawn to that area."

That particular area of the locker room is called "D-Block." And when Moore and Adams recalled linebacker Mike Peterson, in the season prior, calling out that "Everyone wants to come to D-Block," an idea blossomed.

Instead of a player show, Moore wanted to somehow feature the entire area of the locker room—all of D-Block.

"I wanted fans to be able to see that," said Moore. "I'm excited that I get to see it. It was fun for me to watch; I know our fans would do anything to be able to come see this."

Moore approached Peterson in training camp and pitched his idea. He wanted to feature D-Block in some sort of talk-show-type atmosphere, including the entire linebacker corps along with guests from the team.

Moore recalled Peterson's exact response: "Ahhh, yeah, I like that," Peterson said. "I like that a lot. Let's do it."

Live from the D-Block was born, but the editorial direction of the show took a unique direction. Instead of Moore and his video staff taking control of the show, Peterson ran with the idea and took full editorial ownership. D-Block was going to run things. D-Block was going to pick the guests, decide how the program flowed, even design their own set.

The set was still in the linebackers area of the Falcons locker room, but D-Block wanted to give a comfortable feel to the show. They decided to bring in milk crates as seats to, as Moore put it, "make it feel like a front-porch scene."

But that's not all. Each guest was going to have refreshments offered. Since the webisode was filmed directly after practice on Friday, the refreshment of choice was Gatorade. The linebackers had a tub of Gatorade, on ice, for every guest that stopped by. And there were a bunch of guests.

Matt Ryan stopped by and played the guitar. Center Todd McClure was on the show, as were some special guests from the Falcons' past, like Deion Sanders and Jessie Tuggle.

Moore said the webisodes really took off when D-Block invited wide receiver Julio Jones onto the show. The group wanted Jones to tell them something they didn't already know about the rookie from Alabama. Jones was the center of attention at training camp as the Falcons moved up in the 2011 NFL Draft to select him. There weren't too many angles that the media hadn't already dug up. *D-Block* found one.

Jones told the crew that his real name was Quintorris, and that blew the minds of everyone on D-Block. The Internet audience was equally astonished, and Moore said page views went through the roof.

But *Live from the D-Block* was more than just a web show that lots of fans watched. It was becoming hugely popular inside the locker room as well.

As the D-Block crew ran with each episode, more and more of the players would come over to watch. This was never more apparent than when guests Jessie Tuggle and Deion Sanders stopped by.

Moore said his favorite shows still include the Julio Jones episode as well as when Ryan played his guitar and center Brett Romberg sang. But he says, "Deion was fun to watch because those guys went from asking questions to them kind of being in a seminar listening to Deion, taking it all in." And the rest of the locker room hovered.

The same was true for Tuggle, the Ring of Honor linebacker known for his never-stop motor and play-at-top-speed mentality.

When Tuggle spoke, everyone was tuned in. And it wasn't just the linebackers of D-Block. As players finished with post-practice routines, or even in the middle of packing up, they strolled over to D-Block to hear what Tuggle had to say. The moment was quite moving.

"I can remember that in 1991, I finished with 22 tackles against the Saints," Tuggle said after filming the webisode. "The guys asked me about that, and I said, 'You know what, that's when you know you left it all out on the football field.' Whether if you win, lose, or draw. That's what the atmosphere is going to bring for this weekend. I think it's pretty cool to come back and share some of my stories with the current players."

And the fans thought so as well.

Of the top 10 videos on the Atlanta Falcons website, five of them were *Live from the D-Block* shows. "That's incredible," said Moore.

Heading into the 2012 season, Moore said there is every plan to continue shooting the show. The Falcons have even been approached by corporate sponsors that want a piece of the action.

But all those decisions will be made by D-Block. If they want to produce the show again, they will. If they want a corporate sponsor, they'll decide. Moore said the linebackers from D-Block will sit in on every meeting with the sponsors; they'll drive the bus.

In addition to the fellows from D-Block, Moore said he's been approached by a lot of the other position groups on the team. They all want to do a web series like *D-Block*.

The wide receivers want to shoot *Wideout World*, and the offensive linemen want their own show. Moore's agreeable to the ideas but wants them to come up with a different slant.

"No problem," said Moore. "But they can't do a talk show."

60 Catch the Alumni Weekend Festivities

Each season Kevin Winston, the Atlanta Falcons' senior director of player engagement, puts together three days chock-full of activities for alumni of the Falcons. The special events and festivities that make up the annual Alumni Weekend are great for both players and fans.

In 2009 71 former players made the trip back to Flowery Branch for a luncheon hosted by Falcons president Rich McKay. The former players ate and spoke with head coach Mike Smith and general manager Thomas Dimitroff before heading out onto the field to watch practice.

Watching practice is a special moment for the alumni, as well as the players on the field and the media too. This is a time for everyone to mingle and swap stories about the differences between Falcons players and teams of the past and about what's going on now.

In 2009 the topic that overtook the day was breaking the streak of never having back-to-back winning seasons. Former tackle Mike Kenn (1978–94) said his trip back was an attempt to help change misfortunes. "I'm trying to see if they can break the jinx and actually have back-to-back winning seasons, so I am here to support them in that regard," said Kenn.

The Ring of Honor member also praised the Falcons organization. "What I see here is a team that's got a great environment, a great administration, and a good coaching staff. Seems like they're making all the right moves."

Lou Kirouac and former members of teams from early in Atlanta Falcons history joked in an *Atlanta Journal-Constitution* article that they had trouble stringing together back-to-back *wins*, much less entire seasons.

In 2010 more than 100 alumni members showed up for the weekend, which included a tribute to 30 former Pro Bowl Team members who played for the Falcons.

"We're honoring our alumni with a series of events and celebrations this weekend and plan to recognize former Falcons named to the NFC Pro Bowl during their playing days here with our club," Falcons general manager Thomas Dimitroff said. "There are also plans to honor current NFL players who made the Pro Bowl as Falcons during the off-season at the appropriate time."

During these Alumni Weekends there are opportunities for fans to see their favorite Falcons from history. Whether it's at special events or at the game on Sunday—in 2010 the Falcons incorporated Alumni Weekend with Throwback Weekend and had players wearing 1966 uniforms—the Falcons do a great job of getting former players involved with the current team and its fan base.

61 The "I-85 Rivalry"

When the Carolina Panthers entered the National Football League, it was a matter of common sense to place them in the same division as the Atlanta Falcons. For seven seasons the Panthers battled the Falcons in the NFC West division before both teams were recast into the NFC South division.

And why shouldn't these teams be in the same division? Atlanta's home field, the Georgia Dome, sits just 245 miles from the Panthers' Bank of America Stadium on Interstate 85. The Falcons' practice facility is just 208 miles from Bank of America Stadium.

Falcons Take Buses to Charlotte

The drive from Atlanta to Charlotte, at least from stadium to stadium, is 245 miles. That's a short three-and-a-half-hour drive at the speed limit. But the Falcons fly each year and have every time since 1995... except once.

In 2009 the Falcons decided to load up team charter buses and drive from their practice facility in Flowery Branch, Georgia, to Charlotte. And the reasoning behind the switch in transportation mode made sense.

The players typically would converge on Flowery Branch, take buses to the Atlanta airport, and then fly to Charlotte before being bussed to their hotel upon reaching North Carolina. The entire trip would usually take longer that just driving from Flowery Branch to Charlotte.

Head coach Mike Smith told the *Atlanta Journal-Constitution* that the team's support staff had driven to Charlotte for years and always beat the team to the hotel.

"We will get there quicker by taking a bus," Smith said.

The trip was quicker. However, the Falcons lost 28–19 to the Panthers and have not taken buses to Charlotte since.

Not only did their close distance automatically pit the two teams as rivals, but their first game set the stage for hatred.

Carolina's first game as a franchise was at the Georgia Dome against the Falcons. The Panthers jumped out to a quick 13–3 lead before allowing the Falcons to come back and tie the game and send it to overtime. Atlanta survived the expansion Carolina Panthers with a 35-yard Morten Anderson field goal 6:17 into sudden-death overtime.

Panthers owner Jerry Richardson had asked the NFL for a close opener for the Panthers, and his Carolina team got what he wished for—in both distance from home and on the scoreboard.

Beginning with that September 3, 1995, overtime battle, the Panthers and Falcons have played 34 times—twice per year for 17 years. In 14 of those games the winner was determined by a touchdown or less, with the Falcons winning 10 times in that situation.

Early in the rivalry the Panthers and Falcons were pretty even, each team winning five games in the 1990s. But after that, Atlanta started to take over.

The Falcons went 13–7 in the 2000s and haven't lost (4–0) in the 2010s.

62 See a Game under the Big Top

In October, when the weather is pleasant, the football fan takes a last peek at the sunny sky and walks into the Georgia Dome, perhaps a little regretful the game is not being played outside.

In December, when the sky is gray and the air cold, the football fan doesn't bother to look at the sky. They hustle into the Dome, where it is always 72 and pleasant.

Falcons fans cannot have their cake and eat it too, which makes sense when you look at the Dome and its frosting-like dome. The Dome has its good days (when the weather is bad outside) and bad days (when the weather is good outside), and the thing Atlantans have to remember is that their indoor stadium also serves as a host to basketball tournaments, high school football playoff games, tractor pulls, revivals, and all other manner of engines for the economy.

When it was built for the 1992 season, the Dome replaced the multiuse Atlanta–Fulton County Stadium, which was an outside venue that did not have the creature comforts of suites and concession space galore. The Dome was a palace as far as fans were

Postgame at Stats

Be careful when you go in this place before a Falcons game. You might not want to leave.

OK, if it's the Saints or the Giants or the Cowboys, then maybe you're hustling over to the Georgia Dome, which is a deep pass across some rooftops from Stats. But this is the second-best place to make yourself at home for a Falcons game.

You never have to get up...for a beer. Maybe the bathroom, but never for a beer. Stats, which is on Marietta Street down from the Omni Hotel, has self-serve beer taps. I know, dangerous.

It also has 70 HD TVs. No wonder there are so many empty seats near kickoff for Falcons games. I used to think it was fans getting held up at the door for the leg-lift and pat-down by the bomb squad at the gates, but it is fans watching the last speck of pregame shows in Stats, where you can get cheaper and better beer than at the Georgia Dome.

There are seven table taps in six private rooms. The waiter/waitress pouring the beer is the computer.

There is drink, plenty of it, but one of the reasons Stats has been called one of the top 10 bars in the U.S. is the atmosphere and food. Atlanta station 790—the Zone—sometimes broadcasts from the bar, and the remotes are shown throughout the bar. There is plenty of food for adults, but there are also plenty of menu items for children too.

concerned, especially those fans who only spent enough to get a ticket for the upper deck. The upper deck in Atlanta–Fulton County Stadium was exposed to all kinds of weather in the fall and December: rain, snow, sleet, wind, and blazing sun.

The Dome is more than a dry, snug place in the winter. Walk out the front door of the Dome, and MARTA is five minutes away in two directions. It costs $5 for a round trip on the train. Have you seen the premium parking prices around the Dome? $100. What could you do with that extra $95?

The Falcons have still not harnessed the energy of a Southeastern Conference Championship Game crowd. There is not the same hatred for the Saints as there is when Alabama plays Florida. It was noisy for a playoff win over the Rams 10 years ago, and the climax to the winning drive over the Ravens in 2010 brought the house down.

Go soon to the Dome, or you might miss it. The Falcons are angling for a new stadium, and they have brought in the muscle to help them get it. The NFL boss, Roger Goodell, showed up in January 2011 and declared to Atlanta business leaders that the Super Bowl could not possibly be played in a shack like the Dome.

The meaning was obvious: build my friends the Falcons a stadium, or my crown jewel will go to others who do my bidding (Detroit, Dallas, and New York, among others).

The NFL tycoons were knocked off their gilded rockers when there happened to be some ice on the streets of Atlanta for the Super Bowl to close the 1999 season. That was not pixie dust that covered the streets of Dallas in the winter of 2010. It was nasty. The Georgia Dome, on the other hand, was shelter to the high rollers on that bad wintry day.

It will do.

63 Falcons Training Camp 2004: So Close You Could Feel It

When Jim Mora was coaching the Falcons (2004–06), he urged the Falcons to give the fans more access, which meant bringing them right up to the field for training camp. There is not much access to NFL players these days, with security and high fences and walls. NFL teams have too much at stake—money—to let fans get too close.

But Mora and fan surveys declared a need for some interaction. Roddy White—the director of event management for the Falcons, not the wide receiver—had ropes put around the field that separated players from fans by a mere 10 feet.

You wanted to see 300-pound linemen crash pads up close? Here was your chance. Want to catch an authentic NFL football and feel the leather? They flew at you.

"The number-one priority for fans after we reviewed research was they wanted to be closer to the players," White said in 2004. "They wanted to see and feel each of the practice sessions.

"Coach Mora thought the same thing too; he loves the idea. He thought the fans should get closer to the game, and he supported us moving the ropes closer. He suggested we turn the field back to how it was originally to give more fans a sideline seat and get them right on top of the action."

Training camp, which is free and open to the public, usually gets under way in late July. Schedules are posted on atlantafalcons.com.

The same players fans watched for several hours came over to the ropes during that training camp to sign autographs after some practices. Fans had a chance to get their picture with cheerleaders

Atlanta Falcons Training Camp Locations Through the Years

The Atlanta Falcons now hold training camp at the corporate headquarters in Flowery Branch, Georgia. But that hasn't always been the case. Since the team's inception in 1966, the Falcons have called five different locations home to their preseason training camp.

Two of the locations have been in Georgia, and one each in South Carolina, Tennessee, and North Carolina.

2005–11	Falcons Training Facility	Flowery Branch, GA
1999–2004	Furman University	Greenville, SC
1979–98	Falcons Training Facility	Suwanee, GA
1971–78	Furman University	Greenville, SC
1967–70	East Tennessee State University	Johnson City, TN
1966	Blue Ridge Assembly—YMCA Camp	Black Mountain, NC

and mascots. Face painters were on hand to draw footballs, the numbers of fans' favorite players, or maybe even their favorite bird (hint: falcon).

The Gatorade Junior Training Camp was set up. Kids and adults were timed in the 20-yard dash. There was a cheerleading clinic at the Falcons complex.

The Falcons fans hosted movie nights, where an inflatable screen for fans stretched out on the grass. *Remember the Titans* and *Rudy* were two of the movies shown. There were fireworks one night.

The players had water misters, but so did the fans. And fans were allowed to bring their own food.

"Training camp can be tough on the players as they compete for jobs with the team, but when you have a lot of fans out there, it can pick up a player's spirit," White said. "I think the more fans we have, the better it is for the team."

64 Routing the Ghosts in Lambeau

You should have seen all the pregame numbers that said the Falcons were doomed. Brett Favre, the Green Bay quarterback, was 35–0 at home when the temperature was below 34 degrees. But the one stat that weighed more than others was that Green Bay had never lost a home playoff game.

On January 4, 2003, Michael Vick, Jessie Tuggle, and the Falcons defense routed the ghosts of Lambeau Field. It snowed, but it didn't matter. Atlanta won 27–7.

It was a thorough beating. Vick, a 22-year-old quarterback, defied the Lambeau ghosts by leading the Falcons down the field for an opening-drive touchdown. Vick finished the drive with a 10-yard touchdown pass to Shawn Jefferson in the back of the end zone. His passes had zip in the cold, and he never appeared shaken by the Packers, the Packers fans, or the Packers climate. The loud crowd—65,358—was momentarily stunned. They figured their team just had a moment and it would be all right soon.

It never was all right. The Packers did not just have a moment. The Falcons had set a tone and built a 24–0 lead. They caused the Packers' fans to turn on their team with boos.

Vick was dazzling, particularly on one play late in the first half. On third-and-three from the Green Bay 39-yard line, Vick was dead meat, caught on the sideline and with Kabeer Gbaja-Biamila bearing down on him, ready to unload and get the pest out of the game.

Vick dodged the sack, then dodged another. He ran for 11 yards and a first down. Ghosts could not have wrapped him up that night. Vick finished with 64 yards rushing on 10 carries, and the NFL took notice of the next great quarterback in its midst.

The Packers saw Vick's arm strength early in the game, an arm just as strong as their All-Pro Brett Favre's. Vick did not have a dazzling night throwing the ball (13 of 25, 117 yards), but he made enough plays with his feet to make up the difference.

"Michael Vick's a great player, he made some great plays, we couldn't tackle him," Green Bay coach Mike Sherman said. "But their whole team played well. It wasn't just Michael Vick."

The Packers played without the speedy All-Pro safety Darren Sharper, who might have been able to contain Vick on some of his runs that kept drives alive.

"You hear that talk that we have never lost a playoff game here," Favre had said during the week. "That weighs on the opposing team. [They] start to believe, *Well, we can't win here.* We all know that is not true, but our guys start believing we can't be beat. I don't wake up and say, 'Uh-oh, 32 degrees. Somebody is in trouble.' But other people do, I guess."

Michael Vick was not one of those other people. The mystique of Lambeau meant nothing to him that night.

65 5-for-1: Julio

The calls went out to Alabama and they went out to NFL scouts and they went out to friends in the business. The Falcons were doing their homework, which is expected when you are about to do a blockbuster deal...and *this* was a blockbuster deal.

The Falcons were exploring whether to trade multiple draft picks for a weapon for quarterback Matt Ryan and a sidekick for Roddy White. Should they trade up from No. 27 in the 2011 NFL Draft and try and get the sensational Julio Jones, the wide receiver from Alabama?

The Falcons scouted Jones and saw his breathtaking speed and his catches. They found out about his heart on his big day at Tennessee (12 receptions, 221 yards) while playing with taped broken fingers.

All one had to do was walk the sideline at a Bama game to be impressed with his athleticism. Seeing Jones' size, one wondered how a player that big could run so fast.

So after failing to get a deal done with the Bengals to move up and grab Georgia wide receiver A.J. Green, the Falcons jumped for Jones. They took him with the sixth pick overall and traded five picks: their first- (27th overall), second- (59th), and fourth-round (124th) picks in 2011 and their first- and fourth-round picks in 2012.

Jones ran a 4.39-second 40-yard dash in the NFL Combine. The Falcons couldn't stay away.

How did it work out? Jones played in 13 games and had 54 receptions for 959 yards. He had eight touchdowns, which tied Roddy White. He had a burst of speed and obvious acrobatic ability.

But did it work out? Not so far. The Falcons did not advance any further in the playoffs, but it would be unfair to lay that at the hands of a rookie receiver.

Other people, however, will ridicule the Falcons. *Sports Illustrated*'s Kerry J. Byrne of Cold Hard Football Facts had a stinging rebuke for Atlanta following a 24–2 loss to the Giants in the wild-card round of the 2011 playoffs:

"The Falcons failed to study the Shiny Hood Ornament Man Law back in the 2011 draft. So they not only drafted wide receiver Jones in the first round, which is almost always a mistake, but also did the unthinkable to make it happen. They mortgaged their future, trading five draft picks to move up the draft board to grab Jones with the No. 6 overall pick. In other words, the Falcons made other parts of the team worse in the belief that a Shiny Hood Ornament would make the entire Atlanta vehicle run better.

"We knew it was a bad move the moment it happened, especially for a team that went 13–3 the year before but failed to win a single playoff game because of problems that were exposed so badly by the Packers. In fact, we issued *Atlanta a D- in our* Sports Illustrated *draft grades*. So we're not engaging in a little revisionist history. The Shiny Hood Ornament Man Law told us it was an impending disaster the second the deal unfolded."

There was speculation that general manager Thomas Dimitroff didn't make the deal at all, that he was pushed into it by owner Arthur Blank. That speculation surfaced when it was revealed in a book by Boston's Michael Holley that Bill Belichick of the Patriots told Dimitroff not to make the deal.

Sources in the SEC told me Dimitroff was very bullish about the deal before he made it, so I have a hard time believing Blank was the force behind the deal.

Jones is going to be a very good NFL player as long as he stays healthy. He has not stayed healthy. He has stayed banged up, which continues the trend for him that was started in college. Jones had a hamstring injury during his rookie season that limited his production and probably cost the Falcons a win or two.

Did the deal work out? Not yet, but it might.

66 1967, 1968: Back-to-Back Nightmares

The Falocons' second draft? It was a disaster. They had 16 draft picks. None of them stuck with the team long enough to make an impact. None. Looking through the roster for 1971 and beyond shows not a single player from the club's second draft. They picked a guy from a school called Elizabeth City and another player from American International.

Bubba Smith (Michigan State) was taken in that draft, and so were Floyd Little (Syracuse) and Steve Spurrier (Florida).

The one name that stands out is Randy Matson. He is considered one of the greatest shot-putters of all time. The Falcons tried to persuade him to play football, and they picked him in the fifth round of the 1967 draft. He was from Texas, after all. In high school he was a sprinter and hurdler. The guy at one time was 6'5" and weighed 280 pounds. No wonder the Falcons wanted him. It would have been a good pick, if he wanted to play football.

The Falcons took a kicker from Ithaca and a quarterback from North Dakota. I am sure they were ambitious players, but the Packers and Cowboys and Colts and Browns had better drafts.

The other notable name was the last pick, the 17th-round pick: Bill Buckner, the quarterback at Delta State. Nope. It was not Bill Buckner, the Red Sox first baseman, who was a pretty good ballplayer. It was just another Bill Buckner, another guy who did not help the Falcons move forward.

They tried to bring in a star wide receiver, Bernie Casey. He said he wouldn't leave the West Coast and the 49ers to play in Atlanta, and that was that. Casey ended up in Los Angeles with the Rams and was a Pro Bowl player in 1967.

So with no new influx of talent, the Falcons, who had won a startling three games in 1966, went 1–12–1 in their second season.

Atlanta allowed 30 points per game and scored 13. The best thing about the Falcons was watching Nobis and some other true professionals for the Falcons but also getting to see the NFL greats come through Atlanta, such as Baltimore's Johnny Unitas and John Mackey and the 49ers' John Brodie and the Rams' Fearsome Foursome with Merlin Olsen, Deacon Jones, Roger Brown, and Lamar Lundy. Brown replaced Rosey Grier before the 1967 season, so it was not the original Fearsome Foursome, but they were still pretty good and worth the price of a ticket, which was less than $10.

The 1967 season started badly. In Memorial Stadium in Baltimore for the season opener, Unitas and Tom Matte hooked up for an 88-yard score, and the Falcons were down 7–0 and on their way to a 38–31 loss. Future Hall of Famer Unitas threw for 401 yards. It was even worse when Unitas and the Colts came to Atlanta, a 49–7 loss. Unitas completed 17 of 20 passes.

But the Falcons won 21–20 over the Minnesota Vikings, the same Vikings that were about to become very good under Bud Grant. Nobis returned an interception for a touchdown, and a bad season finally had a highlight.

The 1968 Falcons were just a hair better: 2–12. They had a really good punter, Billy Lothridge, who averaged 51 yards per punt in one game against the Steelers. He averaged 44 yards per kick that season.

But the point spread in games was almost as abysmal as it was in the previous season: 28–12. The punting of Lothridge, as you would expect, did not make up for the deficiencies in other areas of the game, which was everything else. The team obviously played hard, given the number of close games, but they were still trying to build, and it was going slowly.

Cannonball Butler was the leading rusher, and he averaged 30 yards per game. Bob Berry and Randy Johnson each started seven games at quarterback, but one could not distinguish himself over the other and claim the starting job; at least, that's what the statistics suggested.

67 1980: What Might Have Been

Dick Vermeil, the head coach of the Philadelphia Eagles in 1980, sought out Leeman Bennett following the season. He offered some salve to the wound, something to help cure the pain of disappointment.

"Leeman," Vermeil said, "I didn't mind facing the Cowboys in the playoffs because I know I didn't want to play you guys. We didn't match up."

The Falcons had finished the season 12–4, which included a 20–17 win at Philadelphia in the regular season. Vermeil wasn't just trying to make Bennett feel good. The Eagles coach knew how good the Falcons were that season. He really didn't want to play them again in the postseason.

The Falcons, the NFC West champions, played the Cowboys and lost a thriller 30–27 in the playoffs. The Eagles played the Cowboys and beat them 20–7 and went on to their first Super Bowl, where they lost to the Raiders.

Before the Falcons' 1998 team that went 14–2 or the 2010 team that went 13–3, there was the 12–4 team of 1980. That was the benchmark for the organization.

Bennett had caused a stir in Atlanta with his fierce defenses that blitzed and assaulted offenses. It was meant to cover up some deficiencies and create some offense and field position.

But there were no smoke and mirrors with the 1980 squad. The Falcons existed on talent, and they had work ethic to match that talent. They lost two of their first three and were 3–3 in mid-October when they took off on a nine-game winning streak.

The defense was still stingy, ranking fifth in the NFL in points allowed, but the offense was catching up. Quarterback Steve Bartkowski was healthy and the Falcons had the second-year running back William Andrews, a fullback who plowed through defenses.

Andrews averaged 4.9 yards per carry in 1980 and ran for 1,308 yards. He caught 51 passes and averaged almost nine yards with every reception. He was a third-round pick out of Auburn, but his production made him seem like a first-round talent.

The Falcons had another second-year back, Lynn Cain, out of the University of Southern California. He rushed for a career-high 914 yards.

No wonder the Eagles and Vermeil did not want to see the Falcons in the playoffs.

The Falcons defense featured the linebackers Joel Williams, Buddy Curry, and Al Richardson. The only familiar face that was missing was Claude Humphrey, the All-Pro defensive end. He was with Philadelphia and led the Eagles with 14.5 sacks in 1980.

The Falcons, believe it or not, were a contender for the Super Bowl. It looked as if they were going to be one step closer in their playoff opener with Dallas. Safety Tom Pridemore intercepted Danny White's pass in the fourth quarter, which set up Tim Mazzetti's 34-yard field goal to make it 27–17.

The Cowboys came back with a 62-yard drive as White threw 14 yards to Drew Pearson with 3:04 left in the game to make it 27–24.

The Falcons took the ball back, and they were ready to put it away facing third-and-one with less than three minutes to play. It was right there for them, and then calamity struck. It was the kind of misfortune the Falcons had endured their first 15 years.

Ed "Too Tall" Jones, the Cowboys' All-Pro defensive lineman, stumbled trying to get set up for the play. He ended up stumbling right into the hole where the Falcons had called a run play.

"We didn't have a blocker for him," Bennett said. "We had the right call with our running back, Lynn Cain, and then that happened. We got stopped and had to punt. They scored and we lost."

The Cowboys did not just score; they scored on a mishap.

Bennett said the Falcons were leading 27–24 in the fourth quarter when the Cowboys got to the line of scrimmage at the Atlanta 23. The Falcons had a blitz called, right into the face of White.

"[Drew] Pearson lined up on the wrong side of the field," Bennett said. "If he had lined up on the right side of the field, he wouldn't have caught that pass.

"I heard White later talking about the play, and he said he just unloaded the ball when the blitz came. Pearson was there to catch it."

And with that, the Cowboys, not the Falcons, played the Eagles the next week for the right to go to the Super Bowl. Philadelphia beat Dallas 20–7 and then went on to play the Raiders, who walked over the Eagles 27–10 in the big game.

The Falcons, it could be argued, would have put up a better fight.

68 1991: Farewell to Outdoor Football

December 15, 1991.

That was the day Falcons fans said goodbye to sunny skies and piercing December rain. That was the day there was no more mud for the Falcons to get dirty in or ice to slip on. That was the day the roof was closed and pro football in Atlanta would be played in the steady comfort of 72 degrees on an always-dry field.

The Falcons went out in glory. They beat the Seattle Seahawks 26–13 before 55,834 and were on their way to the playoffs. They played three more games that season, including two playoff games were on the road at New Orleans and Dallas.

Atlanta–Fulton County Stadium was built in 1965 for $18 million and opened for professional sports business in 1966 when the Braves and Falcons moved in. The first attraction, however, was the Beatles, who held a concert there on August 18, 1965. The Beatles drew 34,000. The Falcons did much better than that in their last appearance, with 55,834. It was their fifth consecutive win.

Singer Wayne Newton was there for the final game at the stadium. And that last game could not have been better scripted. The Falcons' win over Seattle clinched a spot in the playoffs with a 10–6 record. It was their first playoff appearance since the strike-shortened season of 1982.

The Falcons defense was ranked 20th in the NFL, but it had enough to shut down the Seahawks. Seattle quarterback Kelly Stouffer was sacked in the first quarter for a safety. Deion Sanders returned an interception for a touchdown in the third.

The Seahawks managed just 33 yards rushing, and their quarterbacks were sacked five times.

Sanders picked off two passes. The Falcons said after the game it was not a pretty win, but what was so wrong with it? There was a lot of defense, and coach Jerry Glanville was chirping as usual after the game.

He talked about how "we"—meaning he—hadn't come to Atlanta to just be part of a losing cause and then be cast off like other coaching staffs before him.

"When we came here, we didn't come here to get beat up," Glanville told Furman Bisher, the great sportswriter for the *Atlanta*

"2 Legit 2 Quit"

The 1991 Falcons were an eventful team. They saw the arrival of Brett Favre, who did not hang around long, and they made the playoffs for the first time in eight seasons. They had some sensational players, such as cornerback Deion Sanders and wide receiver Andre Rison and tackle Chris Hinton.

It was the last season the Falcons would play in the mud and grime of Atlanta–Fulton County Stadium. They would be moving to the polished and dry Georgia Dome.

They also had a theme song, "2 Legit 2 Quit," an MC Hammer song. Hammer fit right in with this squad, and he was seen on the sideline during several games.

The Falcons were legit. They finished 10–6 and beat the Saints 27–20 in the first round of the playoffs in the Louisiana Superdome. They lost 24–7 to the Redskins the next week, but they had a certain aura about them.

It lasted for a while but not long enough.

Journal-Constitution. "We knew what we wanted to do. And to the people who didn't like it…well, we just don't give a damn, 'cause this is us. Today, yeah, this was definitely our way."

When historic and notable events are mentioned for the stadium, the Falcons are left out. Hank Aaron hit his historic home run (755) to pass Babe Ruth there. But did you know that Aaron's nemesis, Barry Bonds, hit his first career home run in Atlanta?

It was a multipurpose stadium built like many others in the 1960s and early '70s, and it barely had enough space for the football stadium. But the Falcons made it home with its dirt infield and grass stains. What a sight that would be now for an Atlanta football team. Grass stains.

Todd McClure: The Steady Mud Duck

When the Atlanta Falcons' offensive line struggled to start the 2011 season, there were all kinds of alibis. Sam Baker, the left tackle and first-round draft pick, was playing with injuries and not 100 percent. The brawler Harvey Dahl had departed in free agency. That could have been some of it.

But a good part of it was the absence of center Todd McClure, the Mud Duck. His streak of 148 consecutive starts ended when he could not get on the field for the 2011 season opener with Chicago and the second game of the season with Philadelphia.

When McClure returned for the Tampa Bay game on September 25, things did not get fixed right away for the Falcons, but they started to get better. After all, this was a guy who started 16 games per season for nine straight years.

Todd McClure's eccentric personality shone through in his Mohawk.

By November 13 the line had come together well enough, albeit with a new starter at left tackle, that quarterback Matt Ryan had a career-high 351 yards passing against the Saints.

The marauding Saints did sack Ryan.

McClure, who is listed at 6'1" and 296 pounds, has been the hub of the offensive line for years, a veteran with poise who can rally a unit. It is McClure who helps quarterback Matt Ryan identify blitzers and shifts in the defense and how to arrange the blocking play to play.

McClure, who played at LSU, has had quite a career for a player who was picked 237th in the 1999 draft. A seventh-round draft pick, he has survived through three coaching changes and kept an offensive line together in most seasons. He was still around after Dan Reeves was pushed out the door before the end of the 2003 season and replaced by Wade Phillips. McClure survived the erratic coach Jim Mora, who replaced Phillips, and the devastation to the franchise brought by Michael Vick and then the abrupt departure of Bobby Petrino.

The Falcons retooled their offensive line with McClure shepherding undrafted free agents Tyson Clabo and Harvey Dahl. The Falcons allowed a franchise-record low of 17 sacks in 2008 in taking care of rookie quarterback Matt Ryan. They plowed holes for running back Michael Turner, who returned the favor, along with Ryan, by buying the offensive linemen big-screen TVs.

McClure has a son named Maverick, but it is the dad who was somewhat of a maverick, showing up with a Mohawk. The haircuts were fun, but McClure was all business and managed himself like a professional season after season after season.

He was past his prime in January 2012 when he got out on the open market as a free agent. The Falcons still signed McClure to a one-year deal, likely his last. There is value in leadership.

70 The Pro Bowl Lineup

We can pick an all-time Falcons team ourselves or we can use other people's opinions. We'll use our opinion and get together a Falcons team to play a team of Saints, Buccaneers, and Panthers. I can tell you right now which team would win the division if we matched them up in a fantasy game.

No, it isn't the Bucs.

The Pro Bowl Count

Tony Gonzalez is not a Falcon for life, as they say, but he is claimed as one of us now. His 12 Pro Bowl appearances go down for the Falcons (2) and Chiefs (10). OK, it's a stretch, but Gonzalez has played in Atlanta three seasons, so he is a Bird.

It is a stretch to include tackle Chris Hinton, who was an All-Pro here for a season (1991) and is in the Colts Ring of Honor. A great guy who owns a business in Atlanta, he was picked for 11 Pro Bowls in his time in the NFL.

As for the Falcons for life, Jeff Van Note, the hardy center who was nimble and strong, went to six Pro Bowls. Claude Humphrey, the marauding defensive end, was also picked for six Pro Bowls.

When you get to five Pro Bowls, you include the linebacker Keith Brooking, who started going to Pro Bowls in 2001. In fact, Brooking was the lone Falcons representative for three seasons (1999, 2000, 2001). Mike Kenn, the offensive lineman–turned-politician, went to five Pro Bowls.

The linebacker Jessie Tuggle also went to five Pro Bowls, which is an accomplishment when you consider many teams put their best guy right in the heart of the defense at middle linebacker.

Offensive guard Bill Fralic went to four Pro Bowls.

Perhaps the Pro Bowl player for the Falcons to admire more than any other was Elbert Shelley. He was from Tyronza, Arkansas, and was selected in the 11th round of the 1987 draft. He was the 292nd player picked.

Shelley went to four Pro Bowls as a special teams player. That's special.

If you just started at quarterback, the race would be over. Michael Vick over anybody the Bucs can throw out there, even Doug Williams. Even if you were to choose Matt Ryan over Mike Vick, the Falcons would still have the edge with the second-string Ryan.

Tampa Bay has not had a running back as productive as Michael Turner; not even Warrick Dunn, who was a Falcon.

Receivers? The Bucs? Roddy White, Alfred Jenkins, and Andre Rison put to shame the Bucs. Tony Gonzalez is a better tight end than Jimmie Giles and better still than Kellen Winslow. What about the Falcons' Alge Crumpler, who was tabbed for four Pro Bowls? He was a really good tight end.

Tampa left tackle Paul Gruber is hard to beat as an offensive lineman, but the Falcons can run out center Jeff Van Note and tackle Mike Kenn, who played 17 years for the Falcons and made five Pro Bowls.

Bill Fralic was on the All-NFL team of the 1980s.

You think Tampa Bay has the edge on defense? I'll take Deion Sanders over any defensive back the Bucs run out there, including Ronde Barber. Tampa Bay's Derrick Brooks was a beast at linebacker and is a future Hall of Famer. Atlanta linebacker Tommy Nobis is not in the Hall of Fame, but he deserves to be there, and he meant as much to the Falcons as Brooks did to the Bucs. Brooks was a better player, but Nobis gets one of the linebacker spots.

We're not even counting linebacker Keith Brooking, who was picked for five Pro Bowls.

You can take Warren Sapp for the Bucs team as defensive tackle. The Falcons have not had a defensive end like Lee Roy Selmon, though Claude Humphrey and John Abraham are pretty close. John Lynch was a good strong safety but not better than Lawyer Milloy.

Rolland Lawrence was a terrific cornerback for the Birds, but we'll give you Barber at a corner.

So, we have four of 11 starters for the Bucs who were better on defense (Brooks, Sapp, Selmon, Barber).

Kicker? Please. Morten Andersen is the all-time leading scorer in the NFL. Jon Kasay of the Panthers was good but not Mort good. Matt Bryant, who plays for the Falcons now, was a Buc but not better than Mort.

Atlanta's team of All-Pros beats the Bucs.

The Saints? Quarterback Drew Brees and the offensive linemen Willie Roaf and Jim Dombrowski could play for the Falcons. The receivers Joe Horn and Eric Martin? No way. Not over White, Rison, and Jenkins. Horn was second string here. Maybe we can make a case for Marques Colston alongside White.

Reggie Bush and Dalton Hilliard are not better than the Falcons' Turner or Gerald Riggs.

The problem is the kicker. Morten Andersen played for the Saints and he played for the Falcons. He played for the Falcons for eight seasons and for the Saints for 13 seasons. He played for the Falcons in the Super Bowl. Fine, we'll call the position a draw. The Falcons' All-Pro team still wins over the Saints.

71 John Zook/Claude Humphrey: "NFL's Best Defensive End Combo"

Not too many defensive end combinations terrified quarterbacks like John Zook and Claude Humphrey. Just ask former Saints signal caller Archie Manning. In a Week 3 game between Atlanta and New Orleans in 1974, Manning and the Saints altered their game plan specifically so that Zook and Humphrey couldn't do what they did best—wreak havoc on the passer.

The Saints refrained from throwing the ball often as Manning only completed six of 14 pass attempts. This stymied the dangerous duo, and New Orleans came away with a 14–13 win over Atlanta.

"The Humphrey-Zook combination is so good that we played with extra care," Manning told reporters after the game. "We went into the game planning to stay on the ground, confident that our defense would keep the score from getting so one-sided that we'd have to pass."

The Falcons drafted Humphrey with the third overall pick in 1968. A year later, they acquired Zook after the Los Angeles Rams drafted him in the fourth round and traded him to the Philadelphia Eagles, who then dealt him to Atlanta. In 1969 the feared Zook-Humphrey combination was born, and quarterbacks had a lot to worry about.

Falcons coach Norm Van Brocklin once called the fearsome twosome "the NFL's best defensive end combo." Based on comments like Archie Manning's, that might have been a fair assessment at the time.

Zook and Humphrey were quite the tandem, even early in their careers. In the final game of the 1969 season, the Falcons upset the Minnesota Vikings thanks to a stellar defensive play made by both players. With 25 seconds left in the first half, and down 3–0, Zook sacked Vikings quarterback Gary Cuozzo and forced a fumble. Humphrey was there to pick up the ball and run 24 yards into the end zone for the game's only touchdown. Atlanta won 10–3.

Following a dominating defensive effort against New Orleans in the 1973 season opener, Zook said, "Our game plan is to give the opposing team three downs and out and get the ball back to the offense." The two defensive ends always played with the kind of energy as if each play was the last.

In seven seasons with Atlanta, Zook never missed a game. He had a tendency to strip the ball away from offenses, forcing eight fumbles in the seven years he was a Falcon. Zook finished his career by playing four years with the St. Louis Cardinals. Humphrey played in Atlanta for 11 years before being traded to Philadelphia. Though sacks weren't an official statistic at the time, Humphrey reportedly tallied 122 sacks in Atlanta. Humphrey, who was named to six Pro Bowls, earned Defensive Rookie of the Year honors in 1968, with 11.5 of his total sacks coming as an NFL newcomer. Humphrey's been a three-time finalist for the Pro Football Hall of Fame and is a member of Atlanta's Ring of Honor.

72. Falcons' First *Monday Night Football* Experience

The Falcons finally got their turn on *Monday Night Football* on November 30, 1970.

The Falcons played host to the Miami Dolphins, who were in the hunt for a playoff spot at 6–4. Atlanta was 3–5–2 and was looking to play spoiler on its first nationally televised primetime football game.

Dolphins kick returner Mercury Morris set the stage early on Monday night. He returned the opening kickoff 49 yards and then turned a sweep play into a 27-yard gain. Morris later set up the first Miami touchdown with a 40-yard run. Morris punished the Falcons defense all night.

Garo Yepremian kicked two first-half field goals, and Jim Kiick ran the ball into the end zone from one yard out to put the Dolphins up 13–0 at halftime.

Four rushers combined for 111 yards on the ground for the Falcons, and Berry threw for 170 yards, but Atlanta could do nothing with the ball, even though the Falcons controlled it for the better part of the game.

Paul Gipson caught a five-yard pass from quarterback Bob Berry in the fourth quarter to put Atlanta on the scoreboard, but Miami countered with a Larry Csonka one-yard touchdown run with 2:27 to play to ice the game at 20–7.

73 1995: The Falcons' Individual Accolades

The 1995 Atlanta Falcons finished with a 9–7 record and made the playoffs. It was a short playoff run, as the Green Bay Packers tossed the Falcons 37–20 in the wild-card round, but it was a winning season nonetheless.

The record and the playoff game aside, 1995 was a banner year for the Falcons because of a few offensive juggernauts.

For the first time in NFL history, a team finished with four players gaining 1,000 yards. "Ironhead" Craig Heyward rushed for 1,083 yards on 236 carries. He also scored six touchdowns. Three receivers—Eric Metcalf, Bert Emanuel, and Terance Mathis—each compiled 1,000-yard receiving seasons. Metcalf led the way with 1,189 yards on 104 catches. Emanuel and Mathis each had 1,039 yards receiving, Mathis on 78 catches and Emanuel on 74.

Metcalf eclipsed the 1,000-yard mark in Atlanta's 14th game of the season at home against the New Orleans Saints, the first of the group to climb over the peak.

Heyward accomplished the feat next, passing the 1,000-yard rushing mark in the Falcons 15th game against Carolina. Heyward's 81 yards that day pushed him over.

Mathis and Emanuel waited until the final game of the season, and quarterbacks Bobby Hebert and Jeff George seemed to know that they each needed the ball frequently.

Mathis caught eight passes for 84 yards and two touchdowns, the second a game-winner. Emanuel caught seven passes for 86 yards in the game, passing the 1,000-yard mark on a 32-yard pass in the third quarter.

On top of the four 1,000-yard gainers, George threw for 4,143 yards in 1995, becoming the 18th quarterback in NFL history to accomplish that milestone.

The Well-Traveled Quarterback

Jeff George moved on from the Falcons following the 1996 season, and he kept moving and moving. He was not an unruly guy; he was actually pleasant to talk to, even with all the turmoil around him. Still, he had a reputation of being unhappy, and he played for five more NFL teams, including the Raiders twice.

You could see it coming.

He started his college career at Purdue but left after a change of coaches when a run-oriented coach was brought in. He committed to Miami, but he was told he would have to compete for the job like everyone else. George decided on Illinois, which is reasonable. The Illini sounded more sold on him than Miami. If you had just two years left, would you take a chance on Miami and politics interfering with everything?

It worked out just fine. George did so well at Illinois that he was the first overall draft pick of the Indianapolis Colts in 1990. That did not work out so well.

George got into a feud with coach Ted Marchibroda and enraged the local fans. He demanded a trade, and the Falcons were right there willing to take him. June Jones wanted a big arm to run his pass-first offense, and George came over and helped the Falcons to the 1995 playoffs.

The sizzle turned to fizzle. Three weeks into the 1996 season—with Atlanta feeling giddy about the Olympics, another playoff run by the Braves, and George back healthy—the Falcons were a mess.

The sideline rant by George at Jones was captured on national television, and the rest was history. He was dubbed "Furious George," but he was never that way when I talked to him in the locker room. He was sure of himself that he wouldn't allow the chatter about him being an idiot interfere with his own perception of himself.

George departed Atlanta and never regained his status as a top-shelf quarterback. He was out of the NFL in 1996 and began working as a commentator. He was two different people. Off the field, a pleasant dude. On the field, he could be a handful. Such is life.

74 Ovie Mughelli and the Falcons Go Green

After the 2006 season, it was apparent there was a missing piece to Atlanta's running game. The Falcons had one of the most dynamic running quarterbacks the NFL had ever seen in Michael Vick. Running back Warrick Dunn was still producing at a high level, and backups Jerious Norwood and Jason Snelling had showed some potential talent. If Atlanta were to add a top blocking fullback, then the running game would be hard to stop.

Enter Ovie Mughelli, drafted by the Baltimore Ravens in 2003. Mughelli earned a reputation as one the NFL's premier lead blockers after his first four seasons. The Falcons were impressed enough with Mughelli to sign him to a six-year, $18 million contract that included a $5 million signing bonus. At the time, the contract was the highest amount a fullback had ever received in the NFL.

But there is a different side to Mughelli, one that Atlanta fans soon learned about. Mughelli is an environmental activist who devotes much of his free time to educating children on green issues that affect the planet. He established the Ovie Mughelli Foundation, a nonprofit organization that offers programs for children around the Atlanta community.

"With my status as an NFL player, I have the ability to motivate and set an example to being good environmental stewards," Mughelli told the *Atlanta Journal-Constitution* in 2011.

Each month, Mughelli's foundation offers a Green Speaker Series, where he gets Earth-conscious business owners to speak to kids about how to make money while practicing sustainable habits in the workplace. Another event Mughelli's foundation employs is Recycle on the Run, which teaches the importance of recycling in an obstacle-course format. The participant who can recycle materials fastest through an obstacle course wins.

In January 2011 Mughelli donated an Earth-friendly playground and athletic field that utilizes the NewGrass technology to the Ron Clark Academy in Atlanta. The idea was not only to familiarize the children at the school about the environment but to help provide a method to keep them active to prevent childhood obesity.

Ovie Mughelli is a champion of living green. He strives to teach kids about environmental conservancy so that they may make the world a better place.

In addition to his work in Atlanta, Mughelli's foundation also has a chapter in Charleston, South Carolina, the city in which he grew up. In 2011 Mughelli was named the No. 2 Eco-Athlete in the world by PlanetGreen.com.

On September 7, 2008, Mughelli got to show how valuable he was to the NFL as a whole. In the first game of the Mike Smith and Matt Ryan era, Mughelli helped pave the way for Turner to rush for 220 yards and two touchdowns against the Lions in Atlanta's 34–21 victory. For the 2008 season, Mughelli played an integral part in Turner rushing for 1,699 yards and 17 touchdowns, which resulted in Turner earning a trip to the Pro Bowl.

In 2010, when Mughelli was in his eighth NFL season, he was named to his first Pro Bowl. This came during Atlanta's NFC-best 13–3 season that saw seven Falcons earn trips to the NFL's All-Star Game.

With the NFL evolving into a passing league, the number of true blocking fullbacks has begun to dwindle. A lot of teams have opted to go in the direction of a hybrid back, one who can block when needed but also tote the ball when called upon. Mughelli remains one of the NFL's few true blocking fullbacks who demands attention on each down. He's often joked about his need for more carries and touches. But it's clear he's fine with being Atlanta's bruiser leading the way for the running game.

Atlanta Falcons Ring of Honor

On September 19, 2004, the Atlanta Falcons scored 17 points in the fourth quarter to break a 17-all tie and beat the St. Louis Rams. The win was nice, as it was the team's home opener and moved them to 2–0 for the season, but the real reason that particular Sunday was so special compared to any other game day was the festivities that happened before the game and at halftime.

Prior to the game, a small ceremony was held in which team owner Arthur Blank and a few team officials introduced running back William Andrews, quarterback Steve Bartkowski, and linebackers Tommy Nobis and Jessie Tuggle to a few select season-ticket holders.

At halftime a highlight reel was broadcast to the fans in attendance before all four players had their banners raised to the rafters of the Georgia Dome. The inaugural class of the Atlanta Falcons Ring of Honor had been announced.

The team wanted to do the entire ceremony all together at halftime, but the league wouldn't allow them extra time at halftime for the celebration. That's why two shorter ceremonies were needed.

The inaugural class featured two former first-round picks in Bartkowski and Nobis. In fact, Nobis was Atlanta's first-ever draft pick in 1966.

Joining the two first-round picks were Andrews, a third-round pick, and Tuggle, an undrafted free agent signed by the Falcons in 1987.

Not only was Tuggle the only player from the group who was not a draft choice—he's still, to this day, the only member of the Falcons Ring of Honor who wasn't drafted—but he is by far the youngest.

Tuggle told the *Atlanta Journal-Constitution* that he grew up watching Bartkowski and Andrews play and was honored to be inducted with players that paved the way before him. "To be in that first group is awesome," Tuggle said. "Whenever I speak of the Falcons, I speak proudly. That's who I am."

Since that Sunday in 2004, four other Falcons have been inducted into the Ring of Honor at three separate times.

Center Jeff Van Note was the sole member of the 2006 class, inducted 20 years after he retired with six Pro Bowl appearances.

In 2008 the Falcons brought two more members into the Ring. Offensive tackle Mike Kenn and defensive end Claude Humphrey were inducted. Kenn marked the second offensive lineman honored, and Humphrey was the first defensive lineman.

Finally, in 2010, Deion Sanders was enshrined in Atlanta's Ring of Honor. Sanders played in Atlanta for just five years but made the most of his time with the Falcons. In just five seasons, Sanders set 12 franchise records.

While none of the numbers from any of these eight players is currently being used, the Falcons won't officially retire any jersey numbers. The team prefers to honor the player, not the number.

76 Why "Falcons"

A lot of people liked the nickname "Falcons" for the new NFL team. It kept popping up in the radio contest to name the team back in 1965.

About 1,300 people sent in more than 500 suggested names for Rankin Smith's new football team. There was a push for Fireballs and Lancers and Vibrants. That's a scary thought: Vibrants.

It didn't have a chance once Miss Julia Elliott put a teacher's reasoning behind the nickname Falcons. A schoolteacher from Henry County, Miss Elliott sent in the nickname Falcons and was declared the contest winner because she added a powerful phrase with her entry (there were 40 other people who submitted the name Falcons as well): "The falcon is proud and dignified, with great courage and fight. It never drops its prey. It is deadly and has a great sporting tradition."

Reporter Larry Hartstein of the *Atlanta Journal-Constitution* found some other tidbits to go with the naming of the Falcons.

Wrote Hartstein, "Elliott, a speech teacher who coached basketball and quoted poetry, had a bird-related nickname herself. Griffin High School students called her 'Mama Eagle' because of her strong support of the school's sports teams. The school's mascot then was the Eagle."

For winning the contest, Elliott received four Atlanta Falcons season tickets for three years and a football autographed by the players on the inaugural 1966 team. Her seats were excellent, 20 to 30 rows up on the 50-yard line, and Elliott went to nearly every game.

"I don't remember seeing her jumping up and screaming… she was a dignified Southern lady," said her nephew, A. Colvin Moseley of McDonough. "But she'd get real excited about it. She enjoyed seeing people do a good job at whatever they were doing."

77 Visit Heritage Hall

When you walk in the main doors of the Falcons Corporate Office and Training Facility in Flowery Branch, Georgia, one of the first areas that catches your eye is a room off to the left called Heritage Hall.

Upon entering this historical Falcons "vault," the first item that you'll come to is a dinner napkin with writing on it. In true Arthur

Blank fashion—Blank and Bernie Marcus jotted down their idea for the Home Depot on the back of a napkin in 1978—when he met with Taylor Smith, the son of original Falcons owner Rankin Smith, he sealed his intentions to buy the team by writing his thoughts down on his napkin.

"When Mr. Blank gave the formal offer when they were sitting at dinner, he wrote it on the napkin," said Frank Kleha, senior director of media relations. "That's legit; that's what he wrote."

That napkin is encased in Heritage Hall as well as a number of other priceless pieces of Falcons memorabilia.

Fans can see tickets throughout the years; a helmet display from different generations of Falcons teams; a number of areas where they can listen to audio from games, practice, voiceovers from games and videos of special moments since 1966; and much more.

Another special display is the original jersey given to center Tommy Nobis. Nobis was Atlanta's first-ever draft choice in 1966, and the jersey that he was given has been sewed up on numerous occasions.

"Back then they didn't get a new jersey when they ripped them," said Kleha. "They just sewed it back up and they were playing the next week in that same jersey."

In another blast form the past, on display is an actual contract from the Falcons early days, with complete details all the way down to the signing bonus. Incredibly, the contract was typed on paper from a legal pad.

Also located in Heritage Hall is the Falcons' NFC championship trophy from 1998 and an official ball from the 1999 Super Bowl.

78 The Beatdown in the Dome

There has not been a more disheartening loss in Falcons history—not even the Super Bowl loss to the Broncos. This loss, the beatdown at the hands of the Packers in January 2011, was humiliating.

They couldn't have put anything worse on the Falcons' tombstone for the 2010 season. It will hurt when the word is etched into stone and then burned into their résumé by some people. It will absolutely be painful to hear: *Overrated.*

The Falcons came into the NFC playoff game with the Packers that Saturday night with a 13–3 record but dragging a ball and chain called doubt. They had won so many close games that they lacked the look of a dominant team, and it was held against them. Then they went out and got hammered 48–21 by the Packers.

The Falcons beat four playoff teams in the regular season: Green Bay, New Orleans, Seattle, and Baltimore.

"13–3, you can't take that away from us," said linebacker Mike Peterson. "We earned that 13–3. We accomplished a lot of things; we've got a lot of things to be proud of."

What was it then? What happened against Green Bay?

"Tell me," said Sam Baker, the Falcons left tackle, "has anybody answered that question for you tonight?"

Was it mental? The Falcons were the least-penalized team in the NFL that season, but they were flagged seven times in the playoff game. Mike Smith, the Falcons coach, did not think lack of mental toughness had as much to do with the penalties as questionable calls by officials.

Did they have a rattled quarterback? Matt Ryan made poor decisions on several passes. One was poorly underthrown and should have been incomplete in the end zone, but Michael Jenkins slipped on the newly painted NFL logo in the corner of the end zone, and the ball was picked off by Tramon Williams.

On the last play of the first half, Ryan did a half roll out to the sideline. Williams never backpedaled in coverage; he saw the play all the way and jumped the route and intercepted. He took the ball 70 yards the other way for a score.

Were the Falcons overmatched? That is closer to the truth.

Aaron Rodgers, the Green Bay quarterback, was better than the Falcons secondary...by a large margin. The Atlanta secondary is still being built. They need another corner. They missed nickelback Brian Williams, who was injured and replaced by second-year man Christopher Owens. Owens was the nickel early in the season and lost his job in the game against Cincinnati for a reason.

In the quiet of the Atlanta locker room, Roddy White considered what had just happened to the Falcons. And here is the question to ask: did they get some stage fright?

Unacceptable: A Message on a T-Shirt

The 2011 preseason was over, and the Atlanta Falcons were ready to get down to business. The last time the Falcons had taken the field in a game that really mattered, they were blown out of the Georgia Dome by the eventual 2010 Super Bowl champion Green Bay Packers.

Atlanta was the No. 1 seed in that game; the Falcons were the best team in the NFC during the regular season. But the playoffs were another story, and the Falcons were ousted without a postseason win.

Wide receiver Roddy White had T-shirts made for the team and a large number of Falcons players were wearing them in the locker room prior to the team's first practice of the 2011 regular season.

The message on the front was simple and only one word: *Unacceptable.*

On the back of the shirt was written the final score, 48–21, as a reminder that this team should never settle for what happened in the playoffs in 2010.

"It might be something about the big game," White said. "We might not be ready for the stage yet. We might need to go through times like this to get where [we] need to be. Sometimes you need to go through times likes this to see what it's about."

The following season, 2011, the Falcons got in the playoffs again and lost again. They were battered by the Giants, and suddenly the brain trust, coach Mike Smith and GM Thomas Dimitroff, were under fire again.

79 Big-Play Ray Buchanan: The Good and the Bad

Every successful NFL team needs a shutdown cornerback. And in 1997 the Falcons believed they received one in the form of Ray Buchanan.

Drafted by the Indianapolis Colts in 1993 out of the University of Louisville, Buchanan spent his first four years on some decent Colts teams. In his last two seasons with Indianapolis, the Colts finished the regular season 9–7 and earned playoff trips each year. By the time Buchanan decided to leave Indianapolis for Atlanta, he was poised and in his prime.

In 1997 Buchanan started all 16 games for Atlanta at left cornerback and compiled five interceptions and 48 tackles. Buchanan had a knack of coming up with a play when the team needed it most, thus living up to the "Big Play Ray" nickname bestowed upon him. As 1998 rolled around, Buchanan was ready for a monster season.

In Atlanta's first game in 1998, Buchanan recorded his first interception of the season off of Panthers quarterback Kerry Collins. Two weeks later in Atlanta's third game of the season, against San

Francisco, Buchanan picked off another pass, though the Falcons lost the battle 31–20. Buchanan led the Falcons in interceptions in 1998, compiling seven for 102 return yards. He also forced a fumble and recorded 54 tackles. His big-play status helped guide the Falcons to a 14–2 regular-season record, despite his unit ranking 21st in pass defense for the season (allowing 220.7 yards per game). Stout against the run, the Falcons defense gave up yards down the field. But Buchanan and safety Eugene Robinson usually had an opportunistic play waiting, thwarting the opposition's attempt to score points.

After earning the NFC's No. 2 seed, Atlanta defeated the 49ers and the Vikings to earn its first-ever Super Bowl appearance. With the attention honing in on the Super Bowl XXXIII showdown between Atlanta and Denver, it was Big Play Ray's time to shine on Media Day.

With the John Elway–led Broncos heavy favorites, Buchanan showed up in front of the press wearing a rhinestone-encrusted dog collar to hammer home the point that the Falcons were taking pride in being underdogs. At the same event, a reporter asked Buchanan a question about Broncos tight end Shannon Sharpe, and that's when things got testy.

"That's an ugly dude," Buchanan quipped. "You can't tell me he doesn't look like Mr. Ed."

Needless to say, Sharpe took offense and quickly fired back when notified of Buchanan's comment.

"Tell Ray to put the eyeliner, the lipstick and the high heels away," Sharpe said. "I'm not saying he's a cross-dresser; that's just what I heard." Sharpe added, "I've never called anybody ugly. Do I think people are ugly? Yeah, I think he is ugly, but I never said that.... Is he my friend? No. Did I ever view him as a friend? No. Did I view him as an acquaintance? No. Do I like him? No. If I see him in a snowstorm—his truck is broke down, mine is working— would I pick him up? No. Other than that, I could care less about Ray Buchanan."

The war of words gained some traction and gave the nation a reason to talk about Buchanan and the Falcons secondary. But if you're going to risk offering up some bulletin-board material you have to be able to back it up on the field. The Falcons were unable to do so as the Broncos waltzed out of Pro Player Stadium in Miami with a convincing 34–19 win. Elway and the Broncos' passing attack torched Atlanta for 336 yards through the air. Sharpe was held to two catches for 26 yards, but Atlanta had no answer for Broncos wide receiver Rod Smith. Smith caught five passes for 152 yards and a touchdown.

Despite the game's outcome, Buchanan was celebrated as being one of the league's best cover corners that season and earned a trip to the Pro Bowl. But as quickly as success finds you, it can leave your grasp in an instant.

After posting its best season in franchise history, Atlanta succumbed to a 0–4 start in 1999. The press, high on Buchanan just a season before, noted his drop in production. Following a Week 3 loss to the St. Louis Rams, the Associated Press wrote, "The Falcons are winless after three games and Buchanan has been burned on three touchdown passes, in addition to being penalized twice for pass interference and once for illegal contact. 'Big Play Ray' keeps showing up on the wrong side of his nickname."

Buchanan's interception total dipped from seven in 1998 to four in 1999. Atlanta failed to post a winning record from 1999 to 2001. Then the 2002 season rolled around with second-year quarterback Michael Vick breathing offensive life into the franchise. Defensive coordinator Wade Phillips' defense was interception-happy, with picks evenly spread out on the unit. Buchanan stole four passes away and helped Atlanta finish the regular season with a 9–6–1 record. The Falcons were back in the playoffs but fell 20–6 to the Eagles in the divisional round.

By 2003 Buchanan wasn't the kind of player he once was in 1998. After a 1–7 start in 2003, Buchanan was benched in favor of corner Juran Bolden. Following the season, the Falcons released Buchanan, who latched on as a free safety with the Oakland Raiders in 2004. After his one season in Oakland, Buchanan retired from football.

80 Terance Mathis: Great WR, Not-So-Great NASCAR Owner and Potential GM

Terance Mathis has been overlooked at almost every stage of his football career. Growing up in Stone Mountain, Georgia, the University of Georgia and Georgia Tech decided to pass on what many Division I programs deemed too small a receiver to play the position.

Mathis took his playmaking skills to the University of New Mexico, where he became an All-American and the first receiver to catch 250 passes for more than 4,000 career yards—as well as accumulating more than 6,000 total yards. Despite the accolades he earned in college, it still wasn't enough for the 5'10" wideout to earn a sniff on the first day of the 1990 NFL Draft. The Jets finally bit, selecting Mathis in the sixth round. In four years with the Jets, Mathis didn't put up major numbers. His best season was in 1993, when Mathis caught 24 passes for 352 yards.

Despite the paltry numbers, the Falcons decided to take a chance on the Stone Mountain native and signed Mathis, who was an unrestricted free agent after four seasons with the Jets. The gamble paid off immediately. Mathis went from struggling to catch 30 balls in a year with the Jets to hauling in a then–team record 111 passes for 1,342 yards and 11 touchdowns (Roddy White has since broken Mathis' reception record with 115 in 2010).

Proving he wasn't a one-year fluke, Mathis became a mainstay on the Falcons offense. He followed his Pro Bowl 1994 season with a stellar outing in 1995, which saw Mathis catch 78 passes for 1,039 yards and nine touchdowns. In Atlanta Mathis never finished a season with less than 564 receiving yards—and that was as his NFL career was beginning to near an end in 2001.

Mathis played a large role in 1998 when the Falcons reached the Super Bowl. He had 64 receptions for 1,136 yards and 11 touchdowns in the regular season, which complemented fellow receiver Tony Martin's 66-catch, 1,181-yard season. Mathis was also named the NFL's Man of the Year in 1998 for his charity efforts with the Terance Mathis Foundation. After his final season in Atlanta in 2001, Mathis spent a year in Pittsburgh before retiring from the NFL.

Mathis ventured into NASCAR briefly after his NFL playing days ended. In 2005 he founded Victory Motorsports, which featured drivers Morty Buckles and Carl Long. However, by 2007 Mathis was still looking for a sponsor for the team.

"The reason this isn't easy is because, unlike other sports, where the whole league makes sure you're on the right path, in NASCAR you're on your own," Mathis said at the time. "It needs to be fixed."

Though his foray in NASCAR didn't go as he would've liked, Mathis also has another dream he'd like to accomplish one day. At some point, Mathis would like to work his way into becoming the general manager of the Falcons. Of course, Thomas Dimitroff would have to leave his position, and that doesn't appear to be happening anytime soon. But that won't keep Mathis from dreaming.

"My thing is this: I think there needs to be a new breed of general manager out there, and I'm that guy," Mathis told the *Atlanta Journal-Constitution* in 2007. "I can't tell you everything I want to do as a general manager. But after being on the field and getting released, when nobody would return my phone calls, I know there needs to be a connection with players. The NFL is a business, but you're messing with people's lives. If you don't have that connection, you won't be successful as a franchise."

81 Atlanta Falcons As Wrestlers: Bill Goldberg, Bill Fralic, and Roddy White

From one contact sport to another, three famous Falcons in particular have all showcased their athleticism in another venue. Former Atlanta Falcons Bill Fralic (1985–92), Bill Goldberg (1992–94), and current Falcons receiver Roddy White (2005–present) all have experience on some form of a wrestling mat.

The first two mentioned, Fralic and Goldberg, were involved with professional wrestling. After Fralic's rookie season in 1985, he was invited to participate in a 20-man battle royale at the World Wrestling Federation's Wrestlemania 2 event in Chicago. The WWF (now known as World Wrestling Entertainment, WWE for short) also signed on NFL stars William "the Refrigerator" Perry (Bears), Jimbo Covert (Bears), Russ Francis (49ers), Ernie Holmes (Steelers), and Harvey Martin (Cowboys) to participate.

When introduced, Fralic looked sizably smaller than his competition. Then again, everyone looked smaller compared to wrestling's Andre the Giant. The only rule of the match was that a wrestler became eliminated once he was thrown from the wrestling ring and hit the surface below. The first two eliminated from the match, WWF's King Tonga and Covert, fell out of the ring at the same time. Holmes was eliminated next, followed by Jim Brunzell. Slowly but surely, competitors fell from the competition. At one point in the match, Fralic engaged with Andre the Giant, which was certainly a mismatch from a professional wrestling point of view. Fralic escaped Andre the Giant's grasp and then seemed to bounce around, punching and using submission holds at will against anyone he could. But with 11 men eliminated, Fralic was finally thrown from the ring, finishing in ninth place.

Andre the Giant eventually won the WWF-NFL battle royale by defeating the Hart Foundation tag team duo Jim "the Anvil" Neidhart and Bret "Hitman" Hart simultaneously. Andre the Giant first swung Neidhart out of the ring before picking Hart up over his head and tossing him over the ropes onto Neidhart.

In the ring that day, a combined 5,612 pounds' worth of men fought against each other.

Bill Goldberg eschewed professional football for a life in the ring.

Though Fralic is known more for his time with the Falcons, Goldberg has made his name as a professional wrestler. Goldberg was a local product, having played on the defensive line at the University of Georgia. He was drafted by the Rams in the 11th round of the NFL draft in 1990 and was assigned to their practice squad. He later signed a contract with Atlanta and made his debut with the Falcons in 1992, spending three seasons with the franchise and appearing in 14 games. Goldberg's NFL career ended after missing significant time due to a lower abdomen injury.

By 1997 Goldberg had a new career path. While rehabbing his abdomen injury, Goldberg participated in mixed martial arts training and began dabbling in professional wrestling, though it wasn't something he was initially interested in. Goldberg eventually signed with WCW and quickly rose up the ranks. He earned the WCW World Heavyweight Championship belt and built up a 173-match winning streak before suffering his first loss to Kevin Nash, thanks to interference from fellow wrestler Scott Hall.

Though Fralic and Goldberg entered the professional wrestling ring, Roddy White was a high school standout in South Carolina at the traditional and amateur sport of wrestling. White was a two-time state champion who was able to pin an opponent 20 pounds heavier in the Class-AAAA finals with a move he called "the Shanaz."

Even though football got him where he is today, White still enjoys watching wrestling matches and makes appearances on behalf of USA Wrestling when he has the time. ESPN broadcaster Chris Berman sometimes calls White "Rowdy Roddy White" after the professional wrestler Rowdy Roddy Piper.

On the football field, White will use basic wrestling maneuvers to beat one-on-one jams from defensive backs. After all, if you break down football into one-on-one battles, it has a lot of similarities to wrestling, in that the main objective is breaking down the opponent and getting him to the ground.

"Wrestling makes you a better football player," White told *USA Today* in 2011. "It is a great sport for discipline, and it breeds toughness. You learn a lot about individual matchups, quickness, balance, and getting away from guys. It helped me tremendously."

82 Falcons Uniforms Throughout History

The Atlanta Falcons have significantly changed or altered the design of their uniforms five times in the 45-year history of the franchise.

Getting started wasn't an easy task for the Falcons, and it wasn't necessarily civil either.

When the administration at Georgia Tech found out that the Falcons' new uniforms in 1966—the first year of the franchise's existence—were going to feature the red and black colors of their in-state rival the University of Georgia, the Atlanta-based Techies pitched a fit.

The Falcons compromised and added gold and white to the helmets to represent the two college rivals, and the first Falcons uniforms were created.

1966–67

The helmets were red with a black Falcons logo trimmed in white. There were two gold stripes on the helmet (the Georgia Tech compromise). The team wore white pants with a red stripe and black border and wore black jerseys with white numbers.

1968–70

Atlanta removed the Falcons logo from their jersey sleeves in 1968 and replaced it with red and white stripes.

1971–89

The Falcons made the switch to red jerseys in 1971 and wore them for 18 seasons. In 1978 the team switched to silver-gray pants. In 1979 Atlanta added the Falcons logo back to its jersey sleeves, and in 1984 the team changed its face mask from gray to black.

1990–2002

In 1990 the Falcons went back to their roots and wore black jerseys. They also switched to a black helmet with a black face mask. The pants were changed to Falcons silver and had a black stripe down the middle with white and red accent stripes.

2003–Present

In 2003 the Falcons changed their logo to a "more powerful, aggressive Falcon—one of fast movement." The team moved to black jerseys and white pants at home and white jerseys and white pants on the road. In 2004 Atlanta started using a red jersey at home. In 2009, in conjunction with Alumni Weekend, the Falcons wore throwback uniforms from 1966. The team wore them twice that season.

83 Dunta Robinson Comes Home

Dunta Robinson grew up just more than an hour north of Atlanta in Athens, the town most famous for housing the University of Georgia. At a young age, Robinson excelled at football and later became a standout at Clarke Central High School. His abilities made local headlines, and he hoped he would earn a scholarship offer to his hometown college.

As a high school junior in 1998, Robinson thought his dream was coming true. Georgia's coach at the time, Jim Donnan, appeared interested in Robinson and was recruiting him hard. If the offer came, Robinson would most certainly accept.

The offer never materialized, much to Robinson's dismay. He's never forgotten Georgia's lack of interest and always wondered why. He said that during his senior year at Clarke Central, Georgia defensive coordinator Kevin Ramsey rarely called, if at all, and that the Bulldogs dropped his recruitment. Still pursued by other programs in the SEC, Robinson chose to play for the South Carolina Gamecocks, just three hours north of his hometown.

And with South Carolina, Robinson didn't disappoint. As a junior, Robinson picked off four passes and had a team-high 10 pass deflections. He followed his junior year with a stellar senior season that saw his draft stock skyrocket. His eyes were on Atlanta, which was in need of a cornerback and possessed the No. 8 overall pick of the 2004 NFL Draft. But the Falcons spurned Robinson in favor of Virginia Tech's DeAngelo Hall. Robinson went two selections later to the Houston Texans, making him the 10th overall pick. That definitely stuck in Robinson's mind, because growing up he figured he'd have the shot to play for both the Bulldogs and the Falcons.

Robinson's career got off to a fast start in Houston. He started all 16 games his rookie season and picked off six passes. He quickly asserted himself as the best defensive back on Houston's roster and earned Defensive Rookie of the Year honors from the Professional Football Writers of America. Quarterbacks began looking to the opposite side of him, as the interception totals lessened in the years that followed. This wasn't a case of his play dropping off. Robinson was too dangerous to test in man-to-man situations.

But Robinson suffered a setback in 2007 when he tore his ACL in Houston's ninth game of the season against the Oakland Raiders. He missed the remainder of the year and spent 2008 getting back into game shape. Robinson dealt with numerous injuries in 2008, starting only six of the 11 games he played in. By the time the 2009 season was set to begin, Robinson was healthy but not happy. Robinson wanted a long-term deal with the Texans, but Houston would only offer the franchise tender, worth $9.957 million for cornerbacks that season. He held out of training camp in hopes of a new deal, but Houston never offered one to his liking. Robinson signed the tender before the regular season started, and in protest, he wore a pair of shoes that read, "Pay me Rick," in reference to Houston general manager Rick Smith. The NFL levied a $25,000 fine against Robinson for the display.

Robinson finished 2009 healthy, starting and playing in all 16 games. He entered free agency for the first time and wanted to find a team he considered a legitimate postseason contender. One team he was interested in was Atlanta, but since they were disinterested before, why would they be interested now? So when he fielded a phone call from the home-state Falcons brass, it caught him off-guard.

"After not being recruited by the Bulldogs and not being drafted by the Atlanta Falcons, I kind of figured that dream would be over, that it was a dream that wasn't going to come true," Robinson said. "This was totally unexpected. When I got the phone call from Atlanta, I didn't even want to take any other calls from any other teams. I wanted to make that happen. To come and play in front of the hometown crowd, a place where you were raised, it's definitely a dream come true."

Financially, Atlanta made Robinson's wait worth it. In the 2010 off-season, the Falcons signed him to a six-year contract worth $57 million, $22.5 million of it guaranteed. Robinson was coming home and couldn't be happier to do so. While house shopping, Robinson commuted to Atlanta's training facility in Flowery Branch from Watkinsville, a neighboring city outside of Athens, where his parents were living.

Robinson was a key contributor on Atlanta's 2010 defense that finished the regular season 13–3 and earned the NFC's No. 1 seed. His presence forced teams to more frequently test cornerback Brent Grimes, who had a breakout year that ended with a trip to the Pro Bowl. Robinson only picked off one pass and did get beat by receivers some, partially due to Atlanta's philosophy of playing more zone defense than Robinson was used to. Robinson was a matchup, man-to-man corner in Houston and had to go back to the drawing board to learn Atlanta's defense. Robinson has never dodged the media after a poor performance and has admitted his faults when he hasn't played well. When training camp began in 2011, Robinson assessed his production wasn't where it needed to be based on what he was signed on to do.

"If you're going to be in this position, you have to take the good with the bad," Robinson told the *Atlanta Journal-Constitution.* "When things don't go well, I want them to call my name. I want people to say, 'What's he doing to change it?' because that's the kind of player I consider myself—an impact player."

In 2011 Robinson picked off two more passes but still didn't appear as comfortable as the contract he signed made him out to be. Part of it could once again be chalked up to defensive coordinator Brian VanGorder's zone scheme that didn't allow Robinson's talents as a jamming, physical corner to flourish. VanGorder, though, left Atlanta for the same position title at Auburn University after the 2011 season ended. The Falcons replaced him with former San Francisco 49ers head coach Mike Nolan.

Robinson reached his dream of playing with the Falcons but hasn't yet been the star he envisioned. As of the 2012 off-season, Robinson still has time to reassert himself as one of the better NFL matchup cornerbacks.

84 Entire Falcons Team Employs MMA Training after 2009 Season

In the NFL, teams are always looking for a competitive advantage. If it's better training that keeps you stronger for longer and makes you even just a 10th of a second faster, coaches around the NFL are going to jump on board.

With the rise of mixed martial arts in the United States during the 2000s, football players naturally gravitated to the sport's rigorous training and workout regimen. After becoming the head coach of the Falcons in 2008, Mike Smith noticed a handful of his players participating in mixed martial arts training on their own time and away from the team facility. This gave Smith the idea to implement the voluntary team-wide mixed martial arts training program for the Falcons before the 2010 season.

The Falcons hired MMAthletics, a company founded by FOX Sports NFL reporter Jay Glazer and UFC fighters Randy Couture and Frank Trigg. MMA training has helped football players with flexibility in their hips and with gaining leverage against their opponent in man-to-man situations. Atlanta became the first team in the NFL to implement this team-wide off-season voluntary MMA program.

"You get some great conditioning out of it," former Falcons linebacker Curtis Lofton said. "Plus, there's a lot of carryover to what we do on the field. We do some Muay Thai [for core-muscle and hip development], wrestling, working on our hands and getting guys off you. We work on body leverage too, which is important. Whoever is the lowest man controls the other man."

Fifteen to 20 players participated in the off-season program the first year. Players reported that their stamina levels rose through the roof as their conditioning drastically improved. Prior to the Falcons becoming involved with MMA at the team level, San Francisco 49ers linebacker Patrick Willis and Minnesota Vikings defensive end Jared Allen were outspoken about the benefits they received on the gridiron from the mixed martial arts workouts.

Other football players, former and current, have made the leap from football to MMA. Former University of Georgia running back and Heisman Trophy winner Herschel Walker made his MMA debut at the age of 47 in January 2010. Walker defeated Greg Nagy and then followed up with a win over fighter Scott Carson a year later. Baltimore Ravens defensive end Arthur Jones participates in MMA training during the off-season, due to the fact his brother is UFC champion fighter Jon "Bones" Jones.

"This was something we were comfortable with as far as conditioning," general manager Thomas Dimitroff told reporters when the MMA program began. "But even more important [was] the idea of having MMA help the players with their leverage, hand quickness, and things that could help them within the trenches taking on blocks and battling inside."

85 Glanville's Black Uniforms

Jerry Glanville was once football's "Man in Black." When coaching the Houston Oilers in the 1980s, he would wear all black on the sideline, even though his team's colors were powder blue and red. Glanville said he wore all black to make it easier for his players to find him during the hectic motions of an NFL game.

The Man in Black persona made Glanville come across as a bit of a rebel. His Oilers teams had a reputation of hitting hard and playing aggressively. The Houston Astrodome was dubbed the

"House of Pain" due to the Oilers' stingy and aggressive defense, and an altercation with former Steelers coach Chuck Noll became infamous across the league in 1987.

After going 9–7 and losing in the wild-card round of the 1989 playoffs, Glanville accepted a head coaching offer from Atlanta.

Heading into his first season with Atlanta in 1990, Glanville said he inherited a "flat tire" but was determined to fix it. Under Glanville—and because it was the 25th anniversary of Atlanta's existence in the NFL—the franchise decided to make a uniform change.

To go with Glanville's "Man in Black" theme, the team was "Back in Black," wearing the original black jerseys designed for the first-ever 1966 squad. In addition, the Falcons replaced the red helmet with a black one. The pants were silver, whether the team wore a black top at home or a white top on the road. A patch commemorating the team's 25th anniversary was sewn onto the jersey. It was quite the sight to see: the sinister James Dean–looking defensive mind on the sideline with his players fashionably following his lead.

But new uniforms don't guarantee success. That 1990 season was a work in progress, at best. After defeating Glanville's former team, Houston, 47–27 in the season opener, Atlanta lost four of its next five games. After defeating Cincinnati 38–17, Atlanta then lost seven in a row before winning its final two games against the Los Angeles Rams and the Dallas Cowboys. Atlanta finished 1990 a miserable 5–11.

In Glanville's second season—uniforms still intact minus the commemorative patch—the Falcons had much more success. After losing their first two games and beginning the season 3–4, the Falcons won seven of their next nine games to finish the regular season 10–6. They then won a rubber match wild-card round game against New Orleans before falling to Washington 24–7 in the divisional round.

Glanville went 6–10 in 1992 and 6–10 in 1993, which resulted in his firing. Former Falcons quarterback June Jones replaced Glanville at the helm. The Glanville-inspired uniforms remained the same until 1997.

86 Trading Schaub Too Early

There was no way for Atlanta to know that Matt Schaub would become one of the upper-tier quarterbacks in the NFL when the franchise traded him to the Houston Texans for two second-round picks as well as swapping first-round picks in 2007.

It was March 22, 2007, and the Falcons were committed to Michael Vick as the franchise's starting quarterback. Sure, Vick had been inconsistent since being drafted with the No. 1 overall pick in 2001. But the incredible talent was there. Vick led the Falcons to the NFC Championship Game in 2004 and dazzled fans with his athletic prowess. However, questions remained·about Vick's passing game, as he never posted a completion percentage higher than 56.4 percent (2004) with Atlanta. And since he was quick to take off running if his first couple of reads weren't open, he was prone to injury.

Regardless, Vick was the face of the franchise, with billboards plastered around the city. After a 7–9 2006 season, owner Arthur Blank fired coach Jim Mora Jr. and hired Bobby Petrino away from the University of Louisville. Petrino already had a dicey reputation in Louisville because he went behind the administration's back to meet with Auburn University for a head coaching position that wasn't even open yet (Tommy Tuberville was still at the helm of the Tigers). Expressing his loyalty—at the time, that is—Petrino signed a 10-year, $25.6 million deal to stay with Louisville after the 2006 season. That didn't last long, as Petrino bolted to coach the Falcons a few months later.

One reason stuck out among others for Petrino to come to Atlanta: Michael Vick. One Atlanta team representative stated that Petrino was highly optimistic Atlanta would thrive under his system with Vick at the helm. There was a lot of optimism for the 2007 season, which made the Schaub trade acceptable at the time. Schaub wasn't going to start in Atlanta as long as Vick was in town, though Schaub had shown glimpses of his ability to be an NFL starter when placed into game action.

It seemed like a win-win trade at the time. Atlanta would get extra second-round picks in 2007 and 2008 and a higher first-round draft selection in 2007.

But then a month and three days later came. On April 25, 2007, Vick's Virginia home was raided by authorities, who found evidence of an illegal dogfighting operation. By the time training camp was set to begin, the NFL had barred Vick from attending pending its investigation. On August 24 the NFL suspended Vick indefinitely after he signed a plea deal admitting his role in the dog-fighting ring the previous day. Vick would ultimately serve just more than a year and seven months in prison.

From a football standpoint, the Falcons sure wished they wouldn't have traded Schaub away. But hindsight is 20/20, and at the time, it was the right move. And for Schaub, it couldn't have worked out any better. After two promising seasons that ended with injuries in 2007 and 2008, Schaub broke out in 2009 for 4,770 yards and 29 touchdowns for the Texans and was selected to his first Pro Bowl. In 2010 he eclipsed the 4,000 mark again with 4,370 yards and 24 touchdowns.

Atlanta's 2007 season was seemingly over before it started. The Falcons, with Joey Harrington as the team's starter, got off to a dismal 0–3 start before beating Schaub's Texans in Week 4. Atlanta then dropped its next two games to fall to 1–5. Petrino, without telling Harrington beforehand, informed reporters he was benching his starter in favor of Byron Leftwich. The move didn't matter, as Atlanta lost to New Orleans 22–16 with Leftwich sustaining a high ankle sprain. Harrington assumed the starting job again until Week 14, when Petrino benched him again and named Chris Redman the new starter. The Falcons lost that week to the Saints on *Monday Night Football.* Despite the lousy season, Petrino told Blank he was committed to the franchise the day of the Saints game, which was also the same day Vick was sentenced to 23 months in prison. The next day, Petrino left a note on each player's locker stating he was leaving the team. Shortly after, Petrino announced he accepted an offer to become the head coach of the University of Arkansas football program.

Defensive backs coach Emmitt Thomas became the interim head coach, and Atlanta lost its next two games before ending its year with a 44–41 win over Seattle. The horrible season (Atlanta finished 4–12) was over. But things changed in only a year. The Falcons hired Thomas Dimitroff away from New England to be their general manager. Dimitroff then hired Jaguars defensive coordinator Mike Smith to become the Falcons' new head coach. Atlanta then drafted Boston College quarterback Matt Ryan with the third overall pick and never looked back, posting four winning seasons in each of Ryan's first four years at quarterback.

If the Falcons never would've traded for Schaub, you have to wonder where they'd be at this juncture. But then again, the organization and its fans that have moved past the 2007 season are probably OK with what's transpired since.

87 The First Time Ticket Prices Were Raised

These days, football tickets are pricey, even for the bottom-of-the-barrel teams in the NFL. In 2010 the average ticket price for a game was $76.47.

Though times were different, many of the NFL's newest generation of fans would probably be surprised to learn that tickets to Falcons games were $6 each from 1966 to 1970. Tickets to minor league baseball games are now more expensive than what Falcons tickets initially cost.

In 1971 the Falcons decided it was time to increase the cost of attending games. Most seats that had previously cost $6 were raised to $7.50. It may seem like an insignificant amount of money now, but if you were used to a $6 ticket, you probably weren't too keen on paying an extra $1.50 per game. Nonetheless, the Falcons front office felt their product was improving and that it was time to get more from it.

The 1970 team finished 4–8–2 but were extremely close to a winning season despite what the record indicated. In four games, Atlanta held leads into the fourth quarter but couldn't close in the final moments. Atlanta was up on the Los Angeles Rams and the Philadelphia Eagles in back-to-back weeks in the middle of the season but tied both opponents. In Week 2, Atlanta held a 24–20 lead over Green Bay only to see Packers quarterback Don Horn connect with receiver Carroll Dale for an 89-yard touchdown to ultimately win the game. (What made this worse was that Horn came off the bench for Bart Starr and went 1-for-8 passing for the game. His one completion went for the decisive 89-yard score.)

Atlanta also held a 20–14 lead against San Francisco in Week 12 but allowed the 49ers to come back to win 24–20. Signs of promise that Atlanta was turning the corner were evident. And it was time to prove it in 1971.

Through the first five games of the 1971 campaign, the Falcons' idea to raise ticket prices might not have been seen as the greatest concept in the world. The Falcons were 1–3–1, with the three losses coming in Weeks 3, 4, and 5 to the Detroit Lions, the St. Louis Cardinals, and the Los Angeles Rams, respectively. Making matters worse, the losses to St. Louis and Los Angeles both came at home.

But just like that, the Falcons flipped a switch and reeled off wins against New Orleans, Cleveland, and Cincinnati in consecutive weeks to become a game above .500 at 4–3–1. Atlanta then spent the next five weeks alternating between wins and losses. First, the Falcons lost to the Giants. Then they beat the Packers. A loss to the Vikings followed, which was countered with a win against the Raiders a week later. In Week 13 Atlanta fell 24–3 to San Francisco and sat at 6–6–1 with one game remaining on the schedule.

Unfortunately for the home fans, the final game of the season was played in New Orleans. Whether the ticket increase was worth it by the final week of the season couldn't be determined in Atlanta. The Saints weren't having a great season, sitting at 4–7–2 heading into the final showdown against the rival Falcons.

After three quarters, the Saints held a 17–10 lead and were hoping to ruin Atlanta's chances of its first winning season. But running back Art Malone evened the score early in the fourth quarter with a one-yard touchdown run. The Saints added a field goal off the foot of kicker Charlie Durkee from 36 yards away, putting New Orleans up 20–17. Determined to end its season on a high note, Atlanta answered the call. With 40 seconds remaining, quarterback Bob Berry threw a 22-yard game-winning touchdown pass to receiver Ken Burrow. The Falcons escaped New Orleans with a victory and achieved its first winning season, posting a 7–6–1 record.

The record wasn't good enough for a playoff berth, though. The Falcons were beginning to make noise in the NFL but still had to wait until 1978 before reaching the postseason.

88 40,202 No-Shows

There wasn't a lot for Atlanta Falcons fans to cheer about in 1974. After winning two games in early October to move to 2–3 for the season, Atlanta lost its next six games.

Heading into its Week 12 matchup with the Los Angeles Rams, the Falcons were 2–9 overall and had scored just 14 points over their last four games. The team was reeling, and Mother Nature delivered her own blow.

On Sunday, December 1, 1974, 18,648 fans showed up to Atlanta–Fulton County Stadium and saw the Rams destroy the Falcons 30–7. The wind was howling, and the temperature dropped to 33 degrees, keeping 40,202 ticket holders at home.

Team owner Rankin Smith told the Associated Press, "The weather was bad and the team is bad," offering up two excuses for all the empty seats.

But Rams tight end Bob Klein twisted the knife that Smith had already plunged into the backs of fans. "I think Atlanta has some smart season-ticket holders," said Klein.

The 40,202 no-shows set an NFL record that still stands to this day, but it wasn't the only dismal showing of fan support around the NFL. In Chicago, 36,951 ticket holders stayed at home and missed the Bears beat the New York Giants 16–13.

While Atlanta had company on December 1 when it came to the large number of fans that failed to flock to the stadium, the Falcons still have the distinction of having the most.

Atlanta lost one more game the following week before winning its season finale to finish the season with a 3–11 record.

Back to School: John Rade

John Rade was an eighth-round draft pick out of Boise State for the Atlanta Falcons in the 1983 NFL Draft. He became a starter during his rookie season and held that starting job throughout his nine-year career with the Falcons, a career in which he started 112 of his 122 games.

In 1987 and 1988 Rade led the team in tackles, and four times he posted seasons of more than 100 tackles. He was well known for his tenacity on the field and his willingness to tell it like it was.

After a particularly gruesome loss to San Francisco on the road in 1987, the Falcons' 11th loss to only three wins at that point in the season, Rade barked his displeasure to the *Modesto Bee.*

"We played them tough for the first half, then everything went to hell," said Rade after losing 35–7.

"Am I glad this season's over? You bet your ass," Rade continued. "We have to play one last game, and that one's for pride. After back-to-back butt whippings [Atlanta lost 33–0 the week before its 28-point loss in San Francisco], we've got to suck it up. We're all in this together, and we're all screwing up. Our day will come. I don't know when, but it will."

Rade's prophecy of "our day" did come, but it came when Rade was sidelined by injury. The Falcons won 10 games in 1991 and made the playoffs for the fourth time in franchise history. But Rade had injured his right knee in the final game of the 1990 season and had reconstructive surgery shortly after.

The injury got Rade thinking about something other than football for the first time in his adult life, he told the *Atlanta Journal-Constitution.*

"When I had the major operation, I started thinking, *Hey, I'm not invincible.* The knee still gave me a lot of pain, and I knew I had slowed down some," said Rade.

By 1992 Rade had to call his 11-year NFL career quits. He had gone through arthroscopic knee surgery on both knees and said he just couldn't keep up physically any longer.

"When your heart and your brain still work but your legs can't get you there anymore...well, that's a helluva situation to be in," said Rade as he was leaving the team's practice facility and heading home to Boise, Idaho.

Since Rade's body no longer functioned well enough to last in pro football, Rade decided to put his mind to work.

Rade told the *Idaho Mountain Express* that when the Falcons moved him from defensive lineman to linebacker, the transition required him to study and live football. That's where Rade first knew he could master situations with his mind.

With that knowledge, Rade went back to college after his NFL career ended. He took his second go at college much more seriously than his first, when he "majored in eligibility." Rade graduated from Boise State after compiling a 4.0 grade-point average during his second stint in college. He later became a successful business-man, partnering with a former Boise State teammate, but couldn't stay away from coaching football.

When his son, Jared, started playing, Rade got back into coach-ing. He also got into the academic world again. Rade became the

John Rade: an athlete and a scholar.

defensive coordinator for his son's high school football team and also eventually became assistant athletic director.

Rade went from using his body to accomplish his goals to using his mind. In both cases, however, he was very successful.

90 Pat Sullivan: High Expectations Led to Worst Draft Pick of All Time

Quarterback Pat Sullivan was a great college football player at Auburn University. In his 30-game span as Auburn's starting signal caller, Sullivan threw for 6,284 yards and 53 touchdowns. He also ran for 18 scores as well.

Sullivan's biggest accomplishments were rewarded in 1971 when he was named the Heisman Trophy winner.

The Atlanta Falcons were looking for new blood at the quarterback position in the 1972 draft and made deals with four different teams to acquire extra draft picks. They were amazed when Sullivan was still on the board when their second-round pick came along (the 40th overall selection).

Sullivan was taken by Atlanta in 1972 but never was able to win a starting job with the Falcons. In total, over four seasons with the Falcons, Sullivan played in 30 games—25 as a backup and five as a starter. His record as a starter was 0–5.

Sullivan completed less than 43 percent of his passes in the NFL and threw only five touchdowns, compared to 16 interceptions. His quarterback rating was a paltry 36.5.

While still on the Falcons roster in 1975, Sullivan was backup. The man who replaced him was another high-drafted rookie: Steve Bartkowski, the first-round pick of the 1975 draft.

91 What's Said Here... Doesn't Stay Here

Front-office folks should not be in the press box. They just shouldn't be there. One, no cheering is allowed…supposedly. Two, what you say is fair game for reporters.

I've written about the abhorrent scouts in Dallas at the old Cowboys Stadium who would scream at the referees on the field, as if it made a difference. I wrote about the insufferable LSU employees in the old Tiger Stadium press box who pounded on the tables so hard that computers shook whenever the Tigers got screwed by a call.

I wrote about Les Snead, the fine former personnel man for the Falcons, who was hired as the GM of the St. Louis Rams in 2012. He worked his way up from the trenches. Still, when he yelled at the officials or reacted with disgust behind me during several games, I had to react and tell him it was inappropriate. He apologized later. He knew the rules. "I have a lot invested in this team," he said, and I understood. I should have understood then and just moved my seat.

But nobody ever, ever, got out of line like Rankin Smith Jr. in that game in Kansas City. His mistake was that there was a terrific reporter, Glenn Sheeley, within earshot. Sheeley, who is from Pittsburgh and a fair and tough reporter, was fed material for four quarters. It was fair game, a fitting description because Rankin Jr. is a hunter who lives in south Georgia.

The Falcons were finishing up a 4–12 season in 1985, which included a 38–10 loss in Kansas City when Smith could not contain himself. It might not have been the best thing to rip his quarterback and team, but at least Falcons fans understood he was not a dispassionate owner raking in money. He cared.

When quarterback Dave Archer threw a pass over the head of Billy "White Shoes" Johnson on a first-and-20 from the Atlanta 45, Smith muttered, "Great throw, David."

On third-and-20, Archer went past the line of scrimmage and threw an illegal pass. "Dumb," Smith said. "Great play, David."

Smith's disdain traveled to both sides of the ball. When the Falcons' cornerback Wendell Cason dropped a sure interception in the end zone, Smith bellowed, "Oh, you fool!"

On the next play, KC quarterback Todd Blackledge was sacked for a seven-yard loss by Rick Bryan and Mike Pitts. "What? What?" Smith said, feigning disbelief. "I'm glad we got a little rush, because their guys were running free."

When the Chiefs' Stephone Paige gained seven yards for a first down at the Falcons 45, Smith muttered, "Now, don't tackle him."

With the score 24–7, a pass from the Falcons 25 went for four yards to Gerald Riggs. "Great play," Smith said.

Sheeley said Smith pounded the table in the press box and mocked his team.

Atlanta safety Tom Pridemore intercepted a pass with 30 seconds left in the second quarter, and Smith said, "What? What? We intercepted? We should have picked off four passes already."

When the Falcons missed tackles, Smith said, "It's just pathetic."

When the Chiefs went ahead by 21, Smith exclaimed, "This looks worse than last year!"

"I've never seen anything like this," Smith said. "It's just awful."

The moral of the story is that a reporter's job is to get as close to the truth as possible, and sometimes the truth is within earshot. Sheeley's story probably upended fans who thought, *Oh, the Falcons owners just rake in money. They don't care.* They did care.

Sheeley's story also showed frustration that led to personnel changes and a housecleaning. After his outbursts, there was no way Smith could sugarcoat anything with his team. There was news value to the story.

The consequence: "He didn't talk to me for two years," Sheeley said.

92 Press Box Coconut Crème Cake

I am one of 11 children. I eat what's in front of me. My kids mock my tastes and say, "Dad, you like everything."

Maybe, but I think the coconut crème cake in the press box at a Falcons game, served before the game, is amazing. It resets diets ("I'll start again Monday"). There is no self-control. It is not coconut cream pie; it is cake. Believe me, I know the difference between cake and pie.

Anyway, that is one of the trappings of the press box in the Georgia Dome. Here are some other things you might like about the place:

*You get to ask radio analyst Dave Archer what he thinks of the first half and then steal a comment he makes of *X*s and *O*s so that you can ask about it in the locker room after the game.

*Visiting reporters can fill you in on their team. It can contain terrific insight and some of the tawdry stuff they didn't put in their newspaper or on their website.

*You might bump into Jeff Van Vote, who is part of the Ring of Honor. He will give you some insights into offensive line play.

*You can sit next to Len Pasquarelli, the former Falcons beat writer, who has forgotten more football than most of us know. Here's the thing about Len. He is not waiting for you to stop talking so he can tell you what he knows. He's interested in what you know, which he probably already knows.

*The elevator is slow, but I never take it down. There is a stairwell that can get you down to the Floor level and then a right turn and left turn to the Falcons locker room. Some stadiums are a maze. Others make it easy. The Dome makes it easy.

Just don't ask what junk you might run into to get up the elevator before a game. I stood in line for the ride up before one game, then got brushed aside for the commissioner Paul Tagliabue. No one else was allowed on. He went up the elevator with a security man and the NFL PR guy, Joe Browne. There was a lot of room on that elevator.

I took the stairs out of spite and was just fine with it. It's a climb.

93 A Man On Fire

Andre Rison was good. He was really good. He says he was so good that he was better than Jerry Rice. At least, he told the *Atlanta Journal-Constitution* in an interview after he retired that he was better than Rice. That's stretching it a little bit, but he could play.

Rison played for the Falcons from 1990 to 1994. He made the Pro Bowl five times, and in 1993 he led all NFL receivers with 15 touchdown catches. He was a sensational player.

In his career Rison caught 743 passes for 10,205 yards and 84 touchdowns. His 13.7 yards per catch is superb.

Rison averaged 84.6 receptions per season for the Falcons in his five years here.

"Sometimes, I almost think it's a shame that Andre is playing at the same time as [San Francisco's Jerry] Rice or [Dallas's Michael] Irvin," then–Minnesota Vikings defensive coordinator Tony Dungy

An aerial view of Andre Rison's fire-damaged home after it was intentionally set ablaze by Lisa "Left Eye" Lopes.

told the *AJC*'s Len Pasquarelli. "He's one of the great receivers of his era, maybe of any era, and not enough people realize it."

There's more. Rison caught a touchdown pass from Brett Favre in the Super Bowl and got a ring with the Packers.

OK, what you really want to know about is the fire. Fine. Singer Lisa "Left Eye" Lopes, his girlfriend, caused Rison's house to burn down. It was a house he bought for $860,000 that was valued at $2 million. It caught fire in June 1994, and it destroyed all of his possessions.

Lopes was charged with arson. Rison let it slide and even recorded a song with her called "Rags to Riches." Lopes died in 2002.

There are other parts of the Rison story—the failure to pay child support, the Buckhead shooting, etc. But if you want to keep it simple and just think about the football, know this: he is one of the three best receivers in Atlanta Falcons history.

94 Postgame Blather

It is the postgame press conference in the Georgia Dome. The owner sits in the front row, and some other members of the Falcons brass always bring a kid or two. There are some other, gentler folks in the back of the postgame interview room, and there are others who don't belong in the room with the media and Mike Smith when he comes out to talk about a win or a loss.

As you can imagine, it is quite tame in the Falcons' postgame press conference. The owner is in there, so the coach comports himself in a gentlemanly way.

Still, you should see one sometime. You get a televised feed at home, but there is nothing like being there. Smitty is always composed and stays poised throughout the questions that poke at his team or his game plan. I have never seen him lose his temper with a question. Then again, maybe I would have a better chance if the owner wasn't looking right at him, legs crossed, chin up.

Smith, the Falcons coach, will give some decent insight. He can't always say what he wants to say in mixed company, and I bet his postgame interview sessions would be more beneficial if—I said this already…twice—the owner was not there.

It's a show of support, I guess, by Arthur Blank that he is in the room when the Falcons' coach talks about the game. There are only eight of these games that matter each season, so the owner is always on hand. I don't see the owners of other teams in the interview room. Sometimes, not always.

The real electricity and sound bites usually come out of the players' side of the locker room. One locker, in particular. Yes, that would be Roddy White. He is the best at telling you what's on his mind. Never fails. Tony Gonzalez is a diplomat. Roddy is an assassin. Oh, not always, but a lot of times.

When the team stinks, Roddy doesn't dust off a nice cliché. He says, "We stunk, I stunk, we all stunk."

I love him for that. He is the Chipper Jones of the Birds locker room after a game. With some players, you have to wait until the crowd thins out sometimes to get a good nugget because players tend to be less guarded when a camera is not stuck in their face. Not with Roddy. You can wheel 20 cameras in front of him, and he will talk like it's one-on-one with Barbara Walters.

They bring Matt Ryan to the podium in a separate room, but he's still young and not brash at all, so it's hard to get much. Ryan would probably rather kiss a hot iron than talk to the media after the game. His answers will not provoke anyone. He's a great guy, a gentleman, but he doesn't give it much of an effort. I think he has rehearsed a lot of answers on his way in. Maybe the questions are boring.

Of course, the one thing about Ryan is that he will say, point blank, "I played badly" when he played badly. I just want him to get a little deeper with answers and give out some more *X*s and *O*s. By the time he leads the Falcons to a Super Bowl, he will be an ace at the podium.

Now, the real guys to talk to after a game? Offensive linemen. Bob Whitfield was one smart guy. He went to Stanford, I think. Tyson Clabo, a Wake Forest guy, had some insight. Todd McClure could make things interesting for reporters with his spin on a game. I didn't get here until after Jeff Van Note retired, but he was a heck of an analyst on the radio, so I bet he gave some interesting commentary.

It is like that in a lot of locker rooms, college and pro. The offensive linemen give the best interviews after the game. It's hard to figure. Most of the time they are locked in mortal combat with the defensive linemen across from them. They don't have time to see the field.

It is always a chore to get down the elevator to the Falcons' locker room from the press box. The people who are not on deadline always crowd on first. I don't know who these people are, but some of them are wearing Falcons attire in the press box, which should be prohibited. They are not going to wait for the working folks to go down the elevator. They pile on.

I take the stairs. I would count them sometime, but I am in too much of a hurry to hear Mike Smith and the offensive linemen and, of course, Roddy White.

95 Get Tied In With the Foundation

If you are going to get involved with kids, do it big. That's what the Falcons did. They jumped in with both feet. They didn't just write a check, either. They showed up with players and staff. The kids showed up too, when they found out the big names, the NFL players, were going to be in the neighborhood.

In December 2010 Atlanta set the world record for the largest PE class with 2,288 elementary and middle school students around the metro area doing a 30-minute workout routine.

It was not just a publicity stunt. The Falcons have the largest owner-funded foundation in the NFL. They are trying to smother the epidemic of child obesity with both grants and sweat. They have designated Fitness Zones and have lobbied for increased time in physical education classes in school.

Since the Arthur F. Blank Foundation was created in 2002, $18 million in grants have been given. Kids are the target of a lot of the money. After all, it takes money to buy the sports equipment that kids can use for fun and exercise.

The grants also give wider accessibility to healthier foods. Most kids grab the cheapest snack off the shelves and the easiest to reach: the chips, the candy bars.

There are many organizations that stamp themselves as non-profits, and then the money they receive is used to fund an elite travel team of young athletes who compete across the state or in national events. The Falcons have made it clear the money is not for the athlete who is a star. It is for the child who has been left behind by the coach or the team and needs the exercise just as much as anyone.

That's what happens in athletics. The kid with two left feet is the one who needs the attention and the work. One of the goals is to get equipment donated so it can be used for school-aged children. It's not just footballs, basketballs, and baseballs. It can be nets for volleyball, pads for soccer, goals for soccer, and new rims for dilapidated basketball courts that have been bypassed by school funding.

When equipment comes in the door and is made available to kids, they will try it out, and something might stick.

The players and executives showed up to promote healthy lifestyles and physical activity among kids, particularly third through seventh graders who are starting to build habits for adulthood.

"We are excited about the opportunity to continue to spread awareness and emphasize the benefits of exercise and proper nutrition for our young people," Atlanta Falcons president Rich McKay said prior to the event. "We recognize that our players and cheerleaders have significant influence in changing behaviors that lead to childhood obesity, and we look forward to continuing our fight of moving kids from sedentary lifestyles to active ones."

It is easy to find the Falcons youth initiatives online on the team's website. Make a call, make a pledge, or make time. The goal is for kids to exercise 60 minutes per day for five days a week and maintain healthy eating habits.

Of the 100 things to know and do concerning the Falcons, sparing some minutes for the physical fitness of kids should be high on the to-do list.

96 Bill Fralic: The Anti-Steroid Champion

After Bill Fralic's rookie season with the Atlanta Falcons in 1985, the 23-year-old offensive lineman felt the need to call NFL commissioner Pete Rozelle. His message to the commissioner, as Fralic told *Sports Illustrated*: "You've got to do something about steroids. They're a huge problem in this league."

But before Fralic was calling NFL commissioners, he had his own battle with steroids. After his freshman season at the University of Pittsburgh, Fralic's parents found a bottle of pills in his laundry. The pills were a form of steroids called Dianabol. Fralic came clean to his parents but said he needed to continue taking the steroids because "Everybody else is doing them."

Fralic's father had a simple message: "You're crazy! You're big enough and strong enough! You don't need these!"

Fralic stopped taking the drugs but had another battle with steroids later in college. This battle Fralic handled himself. He stopped taking steroids—this time forever—and decided that

Bill Fralic takes a break from game action in what amounted to a 34–17 victory over the 49ers on September 19, 1988, in San Francisco. Fralic was outspoken against the use of performance-enhancing drugs well before the anti-steroid craze began sweeping the nation.

he'd rather fail without taking steroids than succeed by taking them.

Fralic didn't fail. Eventually the No. 2 overall pick in the 1985 draft, Fralic became a starter with the Falcons during his rookie season. In 116 games with the Falcons over eight seasons, Fralic started 115 of them. And he didn't need steroids.

Fralic also felt that no one else in the NFL needed them either. So he became outspoken against steroid use in the NFL. He began, after calling Rozelle, by talking about it openly in the media. He later testified in front of a U.S. Senate Judiciary Committee that 75 percent of all NFL linemen, linebackers, and tight ends used steroids.

Taking his charge further, Fralic was named chairman of the NFL Players Association's drug-prevention committee. He pushed for frequent and random testing in the NFL. Fralic wanted to completely overhaul the NFL drug policy in regard to steroid use.

In many interviews since his retirement from the NFL, Fralic has said that he wasn't sure how his crusade against steroids changed the landscape of performance-enhancing drugs in football. Fralic told the *Pittsburgh Sports Review* that he knew there would always be players trying to get an advantage and that some would look toward illegal methods.

But because Fralic was so outspoken so early on, maybe he changed the course of lives in the NFL. If it was even just one, his efforts were worthwhile.

After his playing career, Fralic called games in the booth. He worked as a color analyst for Atlanta Falcons games for three seasons then moved to call Pitt Panthers games for seven more. Fralic now runs Bill Fralic Insurance Services in metro Atlanta, a company he founded while still playing for the Falcons.

97 The Freak

So go look for it on YouTube or somewhere on the web. Play it back, again and again, and watch the Atlanta Falcons' Brent Grimes, all 5'9" of him, leap and stretch and steal a Drew Brees pass.

The ball was going over his head, and this runt of an NFL defensive back just launched off the turf and intercepted a pass from a quarterback who knows how to get balls over defensive backs.

The other behemoths who play for the Falcons walk off the field past Grimes, and you can see the size difference, and you just have to say to him, "Explain yourself."

Grimes, a cornerback, just smiles. "What do you mean explain myself?" Then he smiles again; he gets it. The height, the leaping ability. Coming from Shippensburg, the small school no one has heard of outside Pennsylvania?

"Yeah, that. What are you doing out here?" It wasn't meant to be disrespectful. It was meant as admiration.

"You should have seen me in high school, smaller than this— 5'6", 5'7", maybe 145 pounds," Grimes said. "I was a running back."

Grimes' father was a baseball player. His father has kin who participated in the Olympics. There are some genetics involved here, but he still went to tiny Shippensburg State, and no one was going to give him a break coming out of that place or give him a chance to make the NFL.

Grimes got a shot as a free agent in 2006, and he kept hanging and hanging. He can jump, but he also pays attention on the practice field when orders are given, and he can take tough coaching.

"He's an acrobat," said John Parker Wilson, one of the backup quarterbacks. "He recovers so fast. That's what he does."

Grimes led the Falcons with six interceptions in 2009. In 2010 he led the team with five interceptions and 23 passes defended, which was a team record. In 2011 Grimes had one interception, which leads one to believe that opponents worked the other side of the field or down the middle.

He is the corner on the one side of the field the Falcons have not had to worry about. They signed a big free agent, Dunta Robinson, before the 2010 season. They signed another free-agent corner, Asante Samuel, before the 2012 season. Meanwhile, the Falcons also drafted Dominique Franks, a big physical corner out of Oklahoma, in the fifth round in the spring of 2010. In 2009 they grabbed Chris Owens, another corner in the third round.

Grimes? He just manages himself on that other side of the field.

Those are the guys who are supposed to be in there before Grimes of Shippensburg, a former practice player. Now he has the big money ($10 million for 2012) as the organization's franchise player.

Grimes is worth seeing in 2012. Take your eyes off the football for a few series and just watch.

98 Visit the Tommy Nobis Center

Every once in a while a football fan, usually a football fan with a gray beard, will walk up to Tommy Nobis, Mr. Falcon, shake Nobis' hand, and thank him for the effort 40 years ago.

"It's neat when I run into an older fan that was here those years. They were teenagers back then. They have a little age on them, like me," Nobis said. "Quite honestly, it is very seldom that I run into a fan of the old Falcons."

Here is the thing about Nobis. His legacy is really not going away with those graying fans. He has left something behind that is more lasting than football.

It is the Tommy Nobis Center. It is dedicated to providing training and counseling to people with disabilities who are usually left at home or in institutions to waste away. Instead of being a tax burden, the Nobis Center helps citizens regain their sense of self-worth and become contributors to the tax base.

In the mid-1970s he was persuaded by Bobbie Knopf and Joyce Slaughter to get involved with them in assisting persons with disabilities.

"Some of my professors and teachers in college told me I was going to have a great opportunity to meet a lot of good people because of playing on a major college team and then going to the pros," Nobis said. "I was taught by my parents to give something back.

"The other thing was, these two Southern ladies approached me, and they were not going to take no for an answer."

The Nobis Center, which is located in Marietta, teaches clients how to fill out job applications and the importance of the interview, but it also teaches real vocational skills. There is assembly work done at the center, and there is a ready workforce to do contract work.

Furman Bisher, the longtime columnist for the *Atlanta Journal-Constitution*, said Nobis was such a solid citizen that life after football did not rob him of significance when the cheering stopped. Nobis admitted he had to take a deep breath when he stopped playing and then take stock.

"After all the bells stopped ringing and the marquee lights grew dim, all did not turn drab for Nobis," Bisher wrote. "There was more of life out there to be lived, something he could give to society. There had been rough edges to be hewn."

"I had to sit down with myself and get hold of myself," he said. "I was a long way from perfect."

Nobis used his superstar status in Atlanta to open doors to funding at the state capitol. In the 35 years the center has been open, it has aided an estimated 18,000 persons with disabilities.

He remains the same in business as he was on the field. Nobis impresses people with effort.

99 2004–2006: The Falcons' Vaunted Rushing Attack

Football games aren't won by individual effort. Sure, one player can shine and put the team on his back, carrying it to victory. But football is still a team game played by 11 players on the field.

Football seasons are also not shaped by the play of one individual. Memorable seasons are put together by groups of players—the Gritz Blitz is a prime example in Atlanta Falcons history.

Groups of players standing out is nothing new. Steve Bartkowski, William Andrews, and Alfred Jenkins formed a threesome in 1981 that lit defenses on fire. Bartkowski threw for 3,829 yards and 30 touchdowns, Andrews rushed for 1,301 yards and 10 touchdowns, and Jenkins tallied 1,358 receiving yards and caught 13 touchdown passes.

In 2011, Matt Ryan, Michael Turner, and Roddy White made up another three-headed monster from Falcons lore. Ryan became the Falcons' greatest single-season passer with 4,177 yards.

Turner passed Gerald Riggs on the all-time Falcons touchdowns list, scoring the 50th of his career in Atlanta. And White became the first receiver in team history to catch 100 or more passes in two consecutive seasons.

So standing out in groups of three is nothing new around the Falcons franchise. But something really special happened from 2004 to 2006 when the Atlanta Falcons were the best rushing team in the NFL.

When mentioning a team that led the league in rushing, most look for a prolific running back that's in the top five statistically. But that's not how the Falcons ruled for those three years.

Warrick Dunn, Michael Vick, and T.J. Duckett became the rushing version of the Atlanta Falcons three-headed monster. And the highest any of them finished in the NFL rankings among rushers for a season was eighth.

In 2004 the Falcons led the league in rushing with 2,672 yards. It was the first time any Atlanta team had ever led the NFL in rushing, and it resulted in an 11–5 record and a playoff berth.

Dunn rushed for 1,106 yards, leading the trio and finishing in 15th place in the NFL in rushing. Vick added 902 yards, while Duckett had 509. Vick, however, was the only one of the three to make the Pro Bowl.

Atlanta rushed for 20 touchdowns that year (third-best in the league) and averaged 5.1 yards per carry (NFL best).

In 2005 the trio got even better, mainly because Dunn upped his game. He ran for 1,416 yards—still just eighth-best in the league—while Vick turned in 597 and Duckett had 380. It was Dunn's first Pro Bowl season since 2000, and the three players averaged 4.8 yards per carry.

The Falcons set a franchise record again in 2006 with 2,939 yards rushing and led the NFL for the third straight season. At that time, the Falcons' 2,939 yards were the ninth-best of all time in league history.

Vick became the first quarterback in the NFL to ever rush for more than 1,000 yards—he tallied 1,039—and Dunn rushed for 1,140. They were only the fourth duo of backfield mates to both land above the 1,000-yard mark in a season.

But it wasn't Duckett who added the change of pace in 2006; it was Jerious Norwood, who rushed for 633 yards.

Vick was no longer with the team in 2007. Neither was head coach Jim Mora, who had teamed with offensive coordinator Greg Knapp to orchestrate the rushing success of 2004–06. Predictably, the rushing game fell off dramatically.

Dunn never eclipsed the 1,000-yard mark again, and the Falcons would have to wait until 2008 and Michael Turner to have another rusher exceed 1,000 yards.

But from 2004 to 2006, no one could pound the rock better than the Atlanta Falcons.

100 Colonel Joe: End With Him

Joe Curtis is blind in one eye and can't see well out of the other, but you will have to pry his Falcons season tickets out of his cold fingers. His seats are on the 50-yard line at the Georgia Dome, which is where an icon should sit. Maybe he can't clearly see Roddy White tiptoe on the sideline after making a catch or Michael Turner plow a defensive back or John Abraham stand over the quarterback after a sack. But "Colonel Joe" is there. He's always there. He's been there since the start.

Curtis, who lives in Macon, has seen every Falcons home game. His season-ticket account number is 33, which is pretty low. Think about it. He was No. 33 in line to get his 10 season tickets in 1966.

"Not sure if there is anybody left that was 1 through 32; they might be gone now," Curtis said. "I have a low number. I'm getting up there in age, you know."

Curtis was 94 in July 2012. As this book went to press, he was making plans to watch the Falcons in 2012. Same seats as usual: 50-yard line, three rows down from the mezzanine concourse. "Of course I'll be there," he said.

He was there when linebacker Tommy Nobis took down his first ball carrier. He was there when the Gritz Blitz gave the franchise something to cheer about and when Gerald Riggs was a workhorse running back and Leeman Bennett was the scheming coach who gave the other side fits.

Curtis was there for the stalwarts on the offensive line—his friend Jeff Van Note and then Mike Kenn and Bill Fralic.

Colonel Joe saw the Falcons in the Super Bowl, and he saw 19 other Super Bowls. He witnessed Michael Vick's fingering of the crowd and the implosion of Bobby Petrino and the rise of Mike Smith and the ownership change from the Smiths to Arthur Blank, who became his friend.

Nothing could knock Joe Curtis off the Falcons bandwagon. Nothing. They were never, ever a disgrace to him, not even in the really pitiful years.

They were his team. They are still his team after 46 years. He was inducted into the Pro Football Hall of Fame in the Fans Exhibit in January 1999 because of his devotion to the Falcons. They picked one fan from 31 teams. The guess is, it wasn't a hard decision to pick Joe.

"It wasn't just home games; I went to a lot of road games too," said Curtis, who was an air force colonel and then a stockbroker. "It's up to 182."

In early April 2012 it was good for Joe to talk about the Falcons because his best friend had just died of liver disease, and Curtis was still in mourning. It took him a few minutes, but he became revved up about the Falcons in that phone call.

When the Falcons moved into the Georgia Dome after the 1991 season, Curtis was allowed to pick out his 10 seats before other season-ticket holders.

He is so into the Falcons that his caretaker these days is none other than the legendary Falcons center Jeff Van Note, who has also been a season-ticket holder since the 1960s.

Curtis proudly says he has photo filed away somewhere that shows Van Note blocking the center and holding two other defensive linemen at the same time. "We had a long-lens camera," Curtis said. "A great picture."

He calls it "absolutely a sin" that Van Note and Nobis have not been inducted into the Pro Football Hall of Fame, and he is not alone among Falcons fans who feel Van Note and Nobis have been cheated.

He loved to watch the high-arching and accurate deep passes by Steve Bartkowski to Alfred Jenkins and Wallace Francis. He calls Bartkowski his friend.

Curtis trusts Mike Smith and has confidence Smith will get the Falcons back to the Super Bowl. Of course, Curtis is the Monday morning quarterback and says Smitty blew the calls going for it on fourth-and-one against the Saints and Giants in the 2011 season.

He wears a Matt Ryan jersey, but he could go into his closet and pull out a jersey of a player from another era if he wanted. Curtis figures he has 50 Falcons shirts in his closet at his retirement home. They share a rack with all his Arnold Palmer shirts.

When he was more fit and feisty, he could back up the good name of Falcons in any bar fight. He didn't like it when the Birds were picked on. So what happened in 1998? He got into a bar fight. He was 80.

"We were down in New Orleans for a game," Curtis said. "I wore my Falcons stuff all over the place, and then I walked into the wrong bar down there, and there were these three Saints guys in there, and they were standing around me, and the guy in the middle said Dan Reeves wasn't worth a toot. I was thinking how I was going to get out of this. I had had a few drinks, I suppose, so I head-butted this one guy in the mouth, and then they were all over me.

"You know where it was? Morten Andersen's old bar. Well, they hit me pretty good and then someone yelled, 'Here come the cops!' and I rolled on the floor and went out the back door."

Curtis made it back to a safe haven of Falcons fans at the Old Absinthe House, and they got him to a doctor and stitched him up. He didn't miss the game.

Speaking about the Saints' recent dilemma with regard to their bounty hunters and suspensions, Curtis said, "I'm not sorry one bit for them."

When Joe does go, his friend, Van Note, will have him cremated and will take his ashes to his boyhood home in Indiana and inter them with Joe's parents.

But Joe is thinking Falcons—not the great beyond—even at 94. He wants to see his team in the Super Bowl again. The 100 miles from Macon are no issue for him. Not after 46 years. All he needs is two tickets—one for him, one for the driver—and he is on his way. He can't wait.

His last words in our interview were, of course, "Go Falcons." And then he hung up.

Sources

Newspapers
- *Atlanta Journal-Constitution*
- *Idaho Mountain Express*
- *Rome News-Tribune*

Wire Services
- Associated Press
- UPI

Magazines
- *Sports Illustrated*

Team Publication
- *Atlanta Falcons Media Guide*

Websites
- Pro Football Reference (www.pro-football-reference.com)
- Atlanta Falcons Website (www.atlantafalcons.com)
- Pro Football Hall of Fame (www.profootballhof.com)
- NFL (www.nfl.com)
- CBS Sports (www.cbssports.com)